HOLIDAY TALES

HOLIDAY TALES

Sholom Aleichem

Selected and Translated by
Aliza Shevrin

DOVER PUBLICATIONS, INC.
Mineola, New York

Bibliographical Note

This Dover edition, first published in 2003, is an unabridged republication of
the text of the work, selected and translated by Aliza Shevrin, originally published
by Charles Scribner's Sons, New York, in 1979 under the title *Holiday Tales of
Sholom Aleichem*.

Library of Congress Cataloging-in-Publication Data

Sholom Aleichem, 1859–1916.
  [Short stories. English. Selections]
  Holiday tales / Sholom Aleichem ; selected and translated by Aliza Shevrin.
    p. cm.
  Originally published: New York : Scribner, c1979.
  Contents: Really a Sukkah! — Benny's luck — A ruined Passover — The esrog —
The goldspinners — The Passover exiles — The first commune.
  ISBN 0-486-42864-8 (pbk.)
  1. Fasts and feasts—Judaism—Juvenile fiction. 2. Children's stories,
Yiddish—Translations into English. [1. Fasts and feasts—Judaism—Fiction.
2. Jews—Ukraine—Fiction. 3. Short stories.] I. Shevrin, Aliza. II. Title.

PZ7.R110Ho 2003
[Fic]—dc21   2002041606

Manufactured in the United States of America
Dover Publications, Inc., 31 East 2nd Street, Mineola, N.Y. 11501

For my beloved parents

RABBI ELIEZER AND RIVKAH GOLDBERGER

A.S.

Contents

Translator's Note

ABOUT once a month a group of us meet to enjoy an evening of Yiddish. We are college professors, townspeople, housewives, some from the old country and others born in America. We share a love for a language fashioned over the centuries to express the longings, passions, delights, and humor of a people who once lived in the small villages, or *shtetls*, of Eastern Europe. At our meetings, we take turns reading stories. When a Jewish holiday approaches, our favorite author becomes Sholom Aleichem, the humorist, satirist, and most beloved of Yiddish writers. It was on his "Tevye" stories that the play and film "Fiddler on the Roof" was based.

Sholom Aleichem, the pen-name of Solomon Rabinowitz, was born in Russia in 1859 and died in New York in 1916. He wrote hundreds of stories which have been read and enjoyed for generations by young and old. It was fitting that he should choose as a pen-name the commonplace, traditional Hebrew greeting, "Peace be with you."

As I was listening to one of his stories for children ("The Esrog"), it occurred to me that although we were adults, we were all responding with the fresh delight of youngsters: chuckling, sighing, laughing, nodding sadly as the story unfolded. I thought, "What a shame that my children and other young people can't enjoy these marvelous tales." True, some are to be found in collections for adults, but I had not seen a book of stories for young readers. This volume is intended to meet that need.

I have selected and translated seven stories with holiday themes. Five have been previously translated and published; two ("The First Commune" and "The Goldspinners") have not been previously published in English. In choosing stories for this collection, I was drawn to the holiday tales, first, because I believe they are among the best stories Sholom Aleichem wrote. Moreover, in telling these stories, Sholom Aleichem accurately showed how Jews celebrated the holidays—not simply as religious observances but as festivals involving the entire family. In these stories we can see and appreciate how all the special customs (the seder at Passover, the sukkah during Sukkos, etc.) were woven into the fabric of family life. Even more important, the stories tell us how individual people experienced these special times of the year, for special they were. They were times to put aside quarrels, worries about poverty, persecution, and hardship. They were times to clean the house from top to bottom, times to get new holiday clothes, times to prepare the holiday dishes, times of togetherness with family and friends, times to commemorate the illustrious past of the Jewish people, and times to thank God for whatever one did have, however little that might be. No one was too poor to celebrate a holiday, even if it meant lighting candles in scooped-out potato shells instead of in silver candlesticks. Whether in one's own house or in an overcrowded apartment, whether in a shed or in an elegant parlor, every person could observe the holidays with equal spiritual merit and emotional fervor.

Not only was Sholom Aleichem a master of Yiddish literature and a great storyteller, he had an intuitive grasp of human nature. He knew exactly how children and their parents would behave. If a mother told her son *not* to do something, as in "The Esrog," that would be the very thing he would be tempted to do. Sholom Aleichem knew that when a youngster gambled away his widowed mother's hard-earned money, he would suffer from acute shame and guilt and have dreams in which he was being punished, as in "Benny's Luck." He knew that when three housewives tried to share the cooking and preparation for a holiday in one kitchen, there would be spite and competitiveness as well as communal spirit, as in "The First Commune."

Although six of the stories are written in the first person from the point of view of a young boy, it is obvious that the boy differs from story to story. In some he has both mother and father, in others only a widowed mother. In some, he is very poor; in others, his family is rather well-off. Sometimes he is an only child and sometimes he has a brother or sister.

I have taken pains to be as faithful to the original language as possible and to render truly every nuance and "untranslatable" idiom or word. In a very few cases extraneous material not considered to be of interest to the young reader has been deleted or condensed. It should be noted that, in the interest of providing variety of setting, the stories in this collection are not placed in the order in which the holidays they describe occur in the calendar year.

However well a translator may do his or her job, a translation is no substitute for the original. I am lucky to have been able to read these stories in Yiddish. I was educated in schools where I was taught to read the Yiddish literary masters in the language in which they wrote. It is my hope that enjoyment of these stories may motivate readers of this book to study Yiddish so that they can read for themselves the truly wonderful works of Sholom Aleichem and other writers as they were written—and aloud, if possible.

The reader's attention is called to the glossary at the back of the book.

I am grateful to my parents, Rabbi Eliezer and Rivkah Goldberger, for a lifetime of living *Yiddishkeit,* encouraged in an environment of scholarliness and love, and for their help in translating archaic and obscure terms. I also wish to thank my editor at Scribners, Clare Costello, for her help and encouragement. My friend Joan Blos provided invaluable support at every stage of the project. Her practical suggestions and knowledge of children's literature were always helpful. In addition, I must thank my friends Louise Kaplan, Shoni and Susie Guiora, Ruth Kirk, and Joseph Blotner for their careful readings and suggestions.

To my children, Dan, Amy, David, and Matt, go my deep regret for failing to teach them Yiddish in childhood, my hope that this collection will help make up for that omission, and my thanks for their encouragement and editorial comments. No words in any language can adequately express the debt of gratitude I owe my husband, Howie, for his loving collaboration in every aspect of this book as in my life.

Aliza Shevrin
Ann Arbor, Michigan
October 10, 1978

HOLIDAY TALES

Really a Sukkah!

During the fall harvest festival of Sukkos, meals are eaten in a home-made shed or lean-to which is covered with leafy branches and is built behind the family dwelling.

T HERE are people who have never learned anything but who can do everything, who have never been anywhere but who know everything, who have never given a thought to anything yet understand everything.

"Golden hands!" That's the name given these people, and the world envies and respects them. Such a man lived in our town of Kasrilevka, and he was called "*Really* Moishe."

We called him "*Really* Moishe" because whenever he saw or heard or made something, he was fond of saying, "That's *really* something!"

Supposing we had a good cantor in our shul. "*Really* a cantor!"

Supposing we bought a big turkey for Passover. "*Really* a turkey!"

Supposing a frost was expected. "*Really* a frost!"

"My friends, you see before you a poor man—*really* poor!" And so for everything.

Moishe was—I can't quite tell you exactly what he was or how he lived. He was a Jew. But how he earned a living would be hard to say. He survived as thousands, shall I say tens of thousands, of Jews survived in Kasrilevka. He hung around the big landowner in town; well, not exactly around the big landowner himself but around those Jews who hung around the *small* landowners who hung around the big landowner. Whether or not he actually made a living was another story because "*Really*

Moishe" was a person who hated to boast about his successes or to complain about his failures. He was always happy, his cheeks were always rosy. His moustache was lopsided, his hat tilted to the side, and his eyes were kind and smiling. Although he was always busy, he could be counted on to walk ten miles to help someone.

That's the kind of man our "*Really* Moishe" was.

There was not a single thing in the world that "*Really* Moishe" couldn't fix—a house, a clock, a machine, a lamp, a top, a spigot, a mirror, a bucket, a cage—you name it.

True, no one could point to the houses or the clocks or the machines that he had repaired, but we were all convinced that Moishe *could* have done it. Everyone used to say that if only he had tools, he could have turned the world upside down. Unfortunately, he had no tools. (Actually, I mean the opposite: it was really lucky he had no tools and the world was not turned upside down.)

It was a wonder that Moishe wasn't pulled apart by all the people who demanded his services. A lock jammed? To whom did one go? To Moishe. A clock stopped? To Moishe. A plugged-up samovar? To Moishe. Cockroaches, beetles, and other nuisances crawling around the house? Whom did one ask? Moishe. A fox stole into the chicken coop and was killing the hens? To whom did one turn for advice? To Moishe. Again Moishe, always Moishe.

True, the jammed lock was eventually tossed aside and forgotten in a closet somewhere, the clock had to be taken to the clockmaker and the samovar to the coppersmith. The cockroaches, beetles, and other nuisances apparently were not terribly frightened of Moishe, and the fox went on doing whatever foxes must do. But "*Really* Moishe" remained the one and only "*Really* Moishe" as before—still "golden hands." I suppose there was some truth in it; the whole world can't be wrong. Here's proof. How come people don't go to you or to me with jammed locks, broken clocks, spigots, cockroaches, beetles, other nuisances, or foxes? Not everyone is alike and talent is, apparently, rare.

It was with this same "*Really* Moishe" that we became very close neighbors, living in the same building under the very same roof. I say "became" because before then, we lived in our own house. But our luck suddenly changed and we came upon hard times. Not wishing to impose on anyone, we sold our house, settled our debts, and moved (it was the night before Rosh Hashanah) into Hershke Mamtzes's house. It was an old ruin of a house, without a garden, without a courtyard, without a porch, without life or soul.

"Let's face it, it's a shack," my mother said with a bitter laugh, and I could see the tears in her eyes.

"Be careful," my father said to her, his face drawn and dark. "Thank God for this."

Why for "this" I don't know. Because we weren't living out in the street? I would rather have been living out in the street than here in Hershke Mamtzes's house. I considered it a great injustice on God's part that He took our house away from us. But even more than the house, I missed the sukkah we had there, a permanent sukkah, one that stood from year to year. It had a flap at the entrance that could be raised and lowered and a beautiful ceiling made of green and yellow branches laid out like Stars of David. Of course, our friends tried to comfort us, telling us that one day we would be able to buy our house back or that, God willing, we would build another one, bigger, better, and handsomer than the old house. But they were no more than words of consolation, cold comfort, just like the words of consolation I heard when I broke (accidentally, of course) my tin watch to bits. My mother had honored me with a spanking and my father dried my eyes, promising to buy me a new watch, bigger, better, and handsomer than the old one. But the more my father extolled the new watch he would buy for me, the more I wept for the old one. Unobtrusively, so my father wouldn't notice, my mother pined after our old home while my father sighed. A black cloud settled over his face and deep creases were etched in his broad white brow. I considered it a great injustice on God's part that He took our house away from us.

"Tell me, if you don't mind, what are we going to do with a sukkah?" my mother remarked to my father a few days before Sukkos.

"I suppose you really mean to say, 'What are we going to do *without* a sukkah?'" my father answered, trying to make a joke of it, but I could see that it was painful for him. He turned away so we couldn't see his face, which had become dark and gloomy. My mother blew her nose in her apron, hiding her tears, and I stood there looking at them both. Suddenly my father turned his face directly toward us and said animatedly, "Wait! Don't we have a neighbor, Moishe?"

"You mean '*Really* Moishe'?" my mother added, and I couldn't tell whether she was joking or serious. Apparently she was serious because within half an hour the three of them—my father, Moishe, and Hershke Mamtzes, our landlord—were outside the house looking for a spot on which to put up the sukkah.

Hershke Mamtzes's house was not too bad a house as houses go, but it did have one fault: it stood too close to the road and had no yard at all. It looked as if someone had misplaced it. Someone had been walking along and lost a house, without a yard, without a real roof, the door on the wrong side, like a coat with the vent in the front and the buttons in the back. If you gave Hershke a chance, he could talk forever on the subject of his house—how they tried to condemn it, how he went to court over the house, how he won his case, and how the house finally remained in his hands.

"Where, Reb Moishe, do you figure on putting the sukkah?" my father asked "*Really* Moishe," and Moishe, hat tilted to the side, was concentrating like a great architect deliberating over an important project and making measurements with his hands from here to there and from there to here. He let it be known that had the house not been placed so badly and had it had a yard, a sukkah with two walls could be built in one day. Did I say one day? In one hour! But since the house had no yard, and four walls would be required, it would take a little longer, but as a result, it would be a *sukkah—really* a sukkah! But most important, the proper material would be needed.

"Material we'll get, but do you have tools?" Hershke asked him.

"Tools can be found, but do you have lumber?" Moishe asked.

"Lumber can be obtained, but do you have nails?" Hershke asked.

"Nails are available, but do you have green fir branches?" Moishe wanted to know.

"Somehow you're very organized today," remarked Hershke.

"Me, organized?" responded Moishe.

They looked at one another and burst out laughing.

When Hershke Mamtzes delivered the first few boards and a pair of wooden posts, Moishe predicted that, God willing, it would be *really* a sukkah. I was very curious to know how he would make a sukkah from these few assorted boards and a pair of wooden posts. I begged my mother for permission to watch Moishe build the sukkah. She agreed and so did Moishe. Not only did he allow me to watch but in fact said that I could be his assistant, which meant I could hand him whatever he needed and hold things for him.

I was in seventh heaven. Imagine, I was helping build a sukkah! And I helped quite a lot. I helped by puckering my lips while Moishe hammered. I helped by joining him for lunch. I helped by shouting at the other children who were underfoot. I helped by bringing him his hammer when he needed a chisel and bringing him his pliers when he needed a nail. Another person in his place would have thrown the hammer or the pliers at my head for that kind of help, but Moishe was a person without malice. No one had ever had the opportunity of seeing him angry.

"Anger," he would say, "is as useful as idol worship. Just as idol worship helps, so does anger help."

Deeply engrossed as I was in the work, I never noticed how and by what miracles our sukkah came to be finished.

"Come, see the sukkah we've built!" I said to my father, pulling him outside by the coattails. My father beamed at our work. Looking at Moishe with a little smile, he said to him, pointing to me, "Reb Moishe, was he any kind of helper at all?"

"He was *really* a helper!" Moishe said, looking up at the roof worriedly. "If only Hershke would hurry up and bring the fir branches, it would *really* be a sukkah!"

❊   ❊   ❊

Hershke Mamtzes was giving us trouble over the fir branches. He put off bringing them from one day to the next till finally, with God's help, the night before Sukkos he rolled up with a wagonload of thin twigs of fir branches mixed with some reeds that grew in the mud on the other side of our pond, and we got to work covering the sukkah. What I really mean to say is that Moishe himself covered the sukkah and I helped drive off the goats which were attracted to the twigs and branches as if they were rare delicacies. I'll never know what they saw in those bitter green stalks.

Since Hershke Mamtzes's house stood all by itself, the goats came from all directions. No sooner did I get rid of one goat than another turned up. I would chase that one away and aha! here was the first one all over again! I drove them away with a stick: "Off with you! Silly goat, are you here again? Off with you!"

The devil knows how they found out we had fir branches. They must have notified one another. How else would all the town goats know to assemble around our house? And I, all alone, had to wage war against them.

With God's help, all the branches were finally on the sukkah roof. Like idiots, the goats stood still, looking up with bewildered eyes, stupidly chewing their cuds. I had triumphed and called out to them, "Why don't you eat the branches now, you silly goats?"

It appeared they understood me because one by one they went off, searching for some new tidbit to eat. Now we got to work decorating the inside of the sukkah. First of all, we spread yellow sand over the ground, then we draped the walls with blankets belonging to the three families who would share the sukkah. When we ran out of blankets, we used shawls, and when we ran out of shawls, we draped a tablecloth or a sheet. Only then did we bring out the tables and benches, the candlesticks and candles, the dishes and silverware. Each of the three women lit her candles and made the blessing on moving into the sukkah.

My mother, blessed be her memory, was a woman who loved to weep. The Holy Days of Mourning were for her a favorite time. From the time we were forced to give up our house, her eyes were never dry. My father, who himself went around in a daze, would not tolerate her tears and told her she should not sin before God because things could be worse, thank God for that. But there in the sukkah, while blessing the candles, she could cover her eyes with both hands and cry quietly so that no one would see that she was crying. But I wasn't someone you could fool. I saw perfectly well how her shoulders were trembling and how the tears trickled through her slender white fingers, falling on the tablecloth. I even knew why she was crying. Luckily for her, my father was preparing to go to shul and was putting on his threadbare Sabbath silk coat and wrapping his woven belt around his waist. He thrust both hands into the belt and with a deep sigh said to me, "Come, let's go. It's time to go to shul to pray." I gathered the daily and High Holiday prayer books, and we went off to shul leaving my mother to pray at home. I knew exactly what she would do first: She would cry. She would have a chance for a good cry! And so it was.

On returning from shul, we entered the sukkah with a big "Happy holiday!" greeting. As my father chanted the blessing over the wine and then sang the kiddush with its beautiful holiday tune, I noticed my mother's eyes, which were plainly red and puffy. Her nose was shiny too. Nevertheless, to me she looked as beautiful as the Matriarch Rachel, or Abigail, or the Queen of Sheba, or Queen Esther. Looking at her, I was reminded of all the beautiful daughters of Zion I had studied about that morning in cheder. As I looked at my fine mother with her pale, pure face, set off by her pretty silk holiday kerchief, with her lovely, large, worried eyes, my heart grieved that such lovely eyes needed to cry so much, that such lovely white hands needed to do the cooking and cleaning. I was disappointed with the Lord above for not giving us enough money. I prayed to God to bring me good luck so that I would find a treasure trove of gold and precious gems. Or let the Messiah come and then we could all go to Israel where it would be wonderful for everyone.

My thoughts carried me far, far away to the place of my dearest dreams which I wouldn't trade for all the wealth in the world. My father's beautiful holiday tune poured into my ears:

Ki vanu vacharta
V'otanu kedashta
Michal ha'amin

I understood the meaning of these words:

Because You have chosen us
And You have blessed us
Above all the nations

That's no small thing—to be a people chosen by God, to be special like an only child. My heart became light and happy because we were the blessed chosen people. I imagined that I was a prince, yes, a prince, and the sukkah was a palace where the Divine Presence resided. Here sat my mother, the great beauty, the Queen of Sheba, and tomorrow, God willing, we would recite the stirring benediction over the best of all fruit, the esrog. Oh, who could compare himself to me? Who could compare himself to me?

After my father's kiddush, *"Really* Moishe" had his turn. It wasn't my father's kiddush but it was all right. And after him the landlord himself, Hershke Mamtzes—an ordinary Jew, an ordinary kiddush. We went to wash our hands and then recited the blessing over the bread. The three women started carrying in the food—the tasty, warm, fresh, seasoned, wonderful-smelling fish—and everyone sat with his family at his own table. There were many loaves of twisted fresh white bread, there were many hands dunking the soft bread in the hot fish broth, there were many mouths eating. A breeze was blowing through the thin, frail walls of the sukkah and through the sparse fir branches. The candles flickered as we all ate, thoroughly enjoying the holiday feast. In my imagination it was still a palace, a stately, brightly lit palace, and we, Jewish princes, aristocrats, the chosen people, were feasting and living in luxury. Blessed be Israel. May you always prosper, O Jews! I imagined myself saying. No people are as fortunate as you. How lucky you are to have the rare honor of sitting in such a fine sukkah, bedecked with green branches and strewn with golden sand and draped with the costliest tapestries in the world. On the table, the holiday loaves and delicious holiday fish were fit for a king.

Suddenly—*Cr-ra-aash!!* The entire roof of green fir boughs dropped right on our heads, followed by the walls one after the other. A goat came flying through the air, landing right on top of us. Suddenly it was dark, the candles blown out, the tables over-turned, and all of us, together with the dishes and goat, sprawled in the sand. The moon shone and the stars twinkled above us. The frightened goat sprang up on its spindly legs, looked around with its guilty eyes like a culprit, and scampered off, leaping impertinently over tables, over benches, and over our heads, bleating "Me-e-eh!" All the candles were out, the dishes shat-tered, the loaves covered with sand, and all of us frightened to death. The women shrieked, the children cried. A shambles! *Really* a shambles!

"That's some sukkah you put up," said Hershke Mamtzes, the landlord, to us afterward, his voice sounding as if we had made him pay for the sukkah, "that one goat could wreck it. Some sukkah!"

"That was *really* a sukkah!" said "*Really* Moishe," looking dumbfounded, trying to figure out just how this all could have happened, "*really* a sukkah!"

"Yes, *really* a sukkah!" mimicked the landlord, and everyone joined in, "That was *really* a sukkah!"

Benny's Luck

Chanukah commemorates the triumphant victory of the small army of the Maccabees over the Syrians many centuries ago. Candles are lit for eight days, potato latkes are eaten, Chanukah money is given, and children play games with the spinning top, or dreydl.

M ORE than all my friends in cheder and more than anyone in the whole town and more than anyone in the world, I loved my friend, Benny Polkovoi. My love was a mixture of real affection, a deep attachment, and more than a touch of fear. I loved him because he was finer, brighter, and craftier than all the other boys. He was devoted and loyal, willing to stand up and fight for me.

I was afraid of him because he was big and quick with his fists. He could beat up anyone at will because Benny was the oldest, the biggest, and the richest boy in cheder. His father, Meyer Polkovoi, even though a tailor with a talent only for sewing army uniforms, was a rich man, a man of means. He had a fine house and a seat at the eastern wall in the synagogue (the third from the Holy Ark). At Passover he could buy the first-blessed matzo, at Sukkos he could afford the finest esrog, on Sabbath he could invite a poor guest to dinner. He gave sizable donations, offered loans without interest, and sent his children to the best teachers. In short, Meyer Polkovoi did everything he could to rise above his station, to become a man to be reckoned with, one of the accepted and respected elders of the congregation—but it was a lost cause! In our Kasrilevka, you didn't just buy your way to the top. In our Kasrilevka, one's status and origins were not so easily forgotten. In our Kasrilevka, a tailor might try to climb the social ladder twenty years in a row, act and dress and live like a rich man, but to us he would always remain a tailor. There was no soap in the world, so to speak, that could wash *that* stain away. But let's get back to my friend, Benny.

Benny was a fine lad, a chubby fellow with freckles, coarse blond hair, pale pudgy cheeks, widely spaced teeth, and remarkable fishlike, bulging eyes. These bulging eyes were always smiling and mischievous. A snub nose accentuated a taunting, impertinent expression. But somehow that face appealed to me. Benny and I became close friends from the moment we met.

Our friendship was really sealed under the table, right in front of the rebbi, while we were studying the Bible. I first met the rebbi when my mother brought me to cheder. We found him sitting with the students as they were studying the Book of Genesis. He was a Jew with thick eyebrows who wore a pointy yarmulke. No time was wasted on entrance examinations or birth certificates. The rebbi just said to me, "Climb around there on that bench between those two boys."

I climbed onto the bench and squeezed between two boys and was considered "enrolled." A conference between my mother and the rebbi was not necessary either; they had made all the arrangements after the holidays.

"Just remember to study hard, like you're supposed to," my mother admonished me as she lingered in the doorway. She turned her head to give me one last look, a look in which I could detect a blend of love, pride, and pity. I understood that look well; she was pleased that I was sitting with studious children, but it also saddened her that we were to be separated.

I must admit that I was much happier than my mother. I was sitting among so many new friends. They were sizing me up and I was sizing them up. But the rebbi didn't let us sit idle for long. He got right down to the business at hand and sang out loud, chanting, motioning for us to repeat after him, and we complied, one louder than the next at the top of our lungs.

V'hanachash—And the snake!
haya—was!
arum—cleverer!
michal—than all!
chayos—the beasts!
hasadeh—of the field!
asher—that!
asah—He created!

Boys sitting so close together, even though they are swaying and chanting, cannot help getting to know each other by slipping in a few words of conversation between the text of the Book of Genesis. And that's the way it was with us.

Benny Polkovoi, who sat right up close to me, tested me first by pinching my leg, then by staring straight into my eyes. Swaying fervently while singing in unison with the rebbi and the rest of the class, Benny began interjecting his own words into the Bible translation without missing so much as a beat,

V'ha-adam—And Adam!
yadah—knew!   (Here, take these buttons!)
et chavah—Eve!
ishta—his wife!   (Give me some carob and I'll let you
                    take a puff of my cigarette!)

I felt someone's warm hand placing several smooth, small, flat trouser buttons in mine. I must confess that I didn't need buttons, I didn't have any carob, and I didn't smoke, but the notion so appealed to me that I answered him in the same chanting rhythm, swaying along with everyone,

V'taher—and she was with child!
v'taled—and she bore a child!   (Who told you I had
                                  carob?)

That was the way we carried on a conversation until the rebbi sensed that despite my pious chanting and swaying, my mind really wasn't on the Book of Genesis. Suddenly he "put me to the wall," by which was meant he was going to test me.

"You there! What did you say your name was? Surely you can tell me whose son Cain was and who Cain's brother was." Since my mind was somewhere else—who knows where?—under the table with the buttons, I suppose, this ridiculous question struck me as crazy, as if someone had suddenly asked, "When will there be a circus in the sky?" or "How do you make cheese out of snow so it won't melt?"

"Why are you looking at me like that?" the rebbi asked me. "Don't you know what I'm asking? I'm asking you and I want an answer. What was the name of the father of Cain, and what happened between him and his brother, Eve's son, Abel?"

I could see all the boys smirking as they tried to keep from laughing out loud. I didn't think there was anything to laugh at.

"You dope, say that you don't know because we haven't studied it yet," whispered Benny in my ear and jabbed me with his elbow. I did exactly as he said and repeated it word for word like a parrot. The cheder boys burst out laughing. "Why are they laughing?" I thought, looking bewildered at them and at the rebbi. They were doubled over with laughter. All the while I was transferring the buttons from one hand to the other; I counted exactly half a dozen.

"Aha! Let's see what you have there in your hands, my young man! What are you doing down there?" demanded the rebbi and bent down to look under the table.

And you can guess what I got from the rebbi because of the buttons on my first day in cheder.

Whippings heal, shame is forgotten. Benny and I became good friends in the best sense of the word *friend*—one soul rather than two. This is how it happened. When I arrived in cheder the following morning with my Bible in one hand and my lunch in the other, I found the boys in a lively, excited mood. How come? Great news! The rebbi was away! Where to? Off somewhere to a circumcision together with his wife, the rebbitzin. Not *together* with her, mind you. A rebbi never goes anywhere *together* with the rebbitzin. The rebbi always goes first, and behind him the rebbitzin follows.

"Let's make a bet!" cried one of the boys with a notable blue nose, Yehoshua-Heshel was his name.

"How much do you want to bet?" replied another, Koppel-Bunim, a lad with a torn sleeve out of which peeked a dirty elbow.

"A quarter of a pound of carob."

"Let it be a quarter of a pound of carob. What are we betting on?"

"I bet he won't be able to stand more than twenty-five."

"And I say thirty-six!"

"Thirty-six? We'll soon see! Grab him, fellows!"

So commanded Yehoshua-Heshel, he of the blue nose, and before I knew what was happening, several boys had grabbed me and laid me down on a bench, face upward. Two of them straddled my legs, two held my arms, one held my head so I couldn't squirm free, and another stuck two fingers of his left hand (he was most likely left-handed) in front of my nose. He made an O with his index finger and thumb, squinted one eye as if taking aim, half-opened his mouth, and started flicking his fingers at my nose. And what painful flicks they were! With each one I saw stars. Fiends! Murderers! What did they have against my poor nose? Whom had it ever bothered? What about it didn't they like? It was a nose like any other nose!

"Start counting, guys!" ordered Yehoshua-Heshel, "One, two, three!" But suddenly—

Ever since the world was created, miracles have happened suddenly. For example, a person is attacked by bandits. They tie his hands up, sharpen their knives, and tell him to say his prayers. Just then, when they are about to do him in, a hunter appears out of nowhere. The bandits take off and the victim is rescued, raises his hands to God in gratitude, and says a blessing of thanks.

That's the way it was with me and my nose. I don't remember all the details, whether it was at the fifth or sixth flick of the nose that the door opened and in came Benny Polkovoi. The gang immediately let me go and each stood rooted to the spot while Benny took care of them one at a time. He gave each boy's ear a good twist as he warned each of them in turn, "Well, *now* you'll know what happens when you pick on the widow's boy!"

From that time on the boys never touched me or my nose. They were afraid of starting up with the widow's boy who had Benny Polkovoi as his friend, savior, and protector.

* * *

"The widow's boy"—that was the only name I was ever known by in cheder. Why "the widow's boy"? I suppose it was because my mother was a widow. She struggled to support herself by running a small shop, mostly selling, as I recall, chalk and carob, two fast-selling items in our Kasrilevka. Chalk was needed for whitewashing houses and carob was a favorite snack because it was sweet, long-lasting, and inexpensive. Schoolboys would spend all their lunch money on these snacks, and the shopkeepers made a good profit from it. I could never understand why my mother was always complaining, claiming she could barely earn enough to pay the shop rent and my tuition. Why was tuition so important to her? How about all the other things a person needs, like food, clothing, shoes, and so on? All she ever thought about was my tuition.

"Since God has punished me," she would say sadly, "and taken from me my husband, and what a husband he was, leaving me alone, a widow with a child, the least I can do is see to it that he has a good education."

How can you argue with that? Don't think that she didn't visit the cheder periodically to check up on how I was progressing. I'm not even talking about saying my daily prayers—she made quite sure that I said them. Her fondest hope was that I would grow up to be the man my father was, may he rest in peace. Whenever she would look at me, she would say that I was altogether "him." Her eyes would become misty, her face worried-looking and full of sorrow.

May my dear father forgive me, I could never understand what kind of a man he was. As my mother told it, he divided all his time between praying and studying. Was there never a time when, like me, he would long to go outdoors on a summer morning when the sun was not yet too hot and just beginning to rise rapidly in the vast sky like a fiery angel in a fiery chariot drawn by fiery horses, so golden bright that it was impossible to look directly at it? What appeal, I ask you, could the daily prayers have, compared to such a magnificent morning?

Who could prefer sitting and studying in a dark, cramped schoolroom while the brightly glowing sun kept on sizzling and blistering the earth like a giant frying pan? That's when more than anything in the world, you yearn to run down the hill to the pond, that lovely little pond sheltered by green branches from which rises a mist that from a distance looks like the vapors rising from the steam bath. That's when you want to throw off your clothes and jump in up to your waist in the sun-warmed pond whose bottom is miraculously cool with slippery soft mud and where a variety of creatures, some half fish, half frogs, glide and float constantly before your eyes. Strange thin-legged insects and familiar dragonflies skate and skitter over the pond's surface. You feel like swimming across to the other side where the broad, round lily pads show off their white and yellow blooms sparkling in the sun. And there above you is a young green willow tree with soft fresh boughs, and you let yourself drop with your hands into the muddy water, kicking your legs up and down behind you, making believe you're swimming.

And what appeal has sitting at home or in cheder in the evening when the bright red ball is descending to earth on the other side of town, igniting the tip of the church steeple and illuminating the shingled roof of the bathhouse as well as the big old windows of the big cold synagogue? On the outskirts of town, herds of goats are scampering, lambs are bleating, the dust is rising higher and higher, frogs are croaking—all creating a busy, tumultuous din. Who can keep praying at such a time? Who could even think of wanting to study at such a time?

But go talk to my mother. She would tell you that he, my father, was never distracted from prayer; he, my father, was a different kind of person altogether. The sort of a man he really was, may he forgive me, is hard for me to say. I only know that my mother pestered me a lot, reminding me constantly that I once had a father like that. She threw up to me at least ten times a day about the tuition she was paying out for me in return for which she was requiring only two things—that I study diligently and pray fervently.

There was no reason to believe that "the widow's boy" was a poor student; he was no better nor worse than any other boy. But as for praying fervently—*that* I couldn't guarantee. All children are alike in some ways, and he was as much a prankster as any of his classmates. Like them, he enjoyed a bit of mischief; like them, he relished acting up at times. Oh, the tricks we thought of: dressing up the town goat in the rebbi's discarded fur hat with which the rebbitzin cleaned house, and letting it run loose in the streets; tying a paper snake to the cat's tail and tormenting her with it until she ran wild, shattering pots or anything else in her way; locking the women's section of the shul from the outside on Friday evening so the women had to be rescued before they fainted; nailing the rebbi's slippers to the floor or sticking his beard with wax to the table as he slept and then just let him stand up! Oh, the smacks we received afterward when it was discovered who had done it—don't ask! Naturally, you can assume that behind every activity there was a ringleader, a guiding spirit, a chief.

Our ringleader, our guiding spirit, our chief was Benny Polkovoi. It was from his head that the ideas originated, but it was on our heads that the blame fell. Benny—the chubby, red-faced Benny with the bulging fish-eyes—somehow managed to squeeze out of every scrape free as a bird, clean as a whistle, innocent as a newborn lamb, even though he was every bit as guilty as any one of us. Every gesture of his, every grimace, witticism, or mannerism was quickly imitated and adopted by us. Who taught us how to sneak a puff on a cigarette, exhaling through our nostrils? Benny. Who talked us into skating on the ice with the peasant boys in town in the winter? Benny. Who taught us how to gamble with buttons, playing cards and checkers till we lost all our lunch money? Benny. When it came to gambling, Benny was a champion. He could beat us all, winning every cent we had, but when it came to trying to win some of it back—*whoosh!* Benny had vanished! Gambling was one of our greatest pleasures and for gambling we earned the worst tongue lashing from the rebbi. He strongly disapproved of gambling and vowed to break us of the habit once and for all.

"Gambling in *my* cheder? I'll have you gambling with the devil!" the rebbi would shout while shaking out our pockets till they were empty, confiscating their contents while meting out blows on all sides.

But there was one week of the year when we were allowed to

gamble. Did I say "allowed"? It was considered a good deed to gamble, a regular commandment! That was the week of Chanukah and we played with the dreydl, the spinning top.

Today's card games and other forms of gambling—poker, roulette, pinochle, and so forth—certainly make more sense than our old dreydl game, but what does it matter as long as money is at stake? Gambling at dreydl can get heated, exciting, and upsetting. It can drive you mad to the point at which you are prepared to sell your soul. It's not so much the money as the keen disappointment: Why did someone else win? Why did the dreydl fall on the winning letter *G* for him and on the losing letters *N, H,* or *Sh* for you? You know what I'm talking about, don't you? The dreydl is a four-sided spinning top with a Hebrew letter on each side. You spin it, and depending on which side it falls when it stops, it tells you whether and how much you've won or lost. *N* means none, *H* means half, *Sh* means shoot again, and *G* means get. The dreydl is really a game of chance. Whoever is lucky, wins. Take Benny Polkovoi, for instance. No matter how many times he spun the dreydl, it always fell on *G.*

"That Benny has all the luck," we boys would say as we put up more money. Benny's response always was "What do you mean, luck? I'm a rich man's son!"

"*G!* Again *G!* What luck!" we screamed all at once as we searched our pockets for more money while Benny, as was his style, spun the dreydl upside down on its thin handle. The dreydl spun around, wobbled back and forth like a drunkard, and fell over.

"*G!*" cried Benny.

"*G?* *G?* Again *G?* I can't believe it!" the boys yelled, scratching their heads and reaching into their pockets again.

The game grew more intense. The participants became more inflamed as they staked their money, shoved one another to get closer to the table, poked each other in the ribs, argued and hurled insulting names back and forth.

"Snotnose!"

"Stutterer!"

"Beanpole!"

"Rag-picker's son!"

With all these compliments flying, we failed to notice that the rebbi had returned and was standing to the side, wearing his warm cap and coat and carrying his prayer shawl under his arm. He was on his way to shul but, hearing all the uproar, had stopped by for a while to look on as we played dreydl. That day the rebbi didn't interfere; it was Chanukah and we were free to play dreydl for eight days in a row, as much as we wanted so long as we didn't fight or pull each other's noses. A sympathetic man, our rebbi. The rebbitzin lifted their small, sickly child, Reuvele, into her arms as she stood behind the rebbi's shoulder looking wide-eyed, taking in our avid gambling. Benny took on all comers, winning everything from everyone. Benny was raring to go, Benny was ferocious, Benny was unstoppable. He spun the dreydl again and again. It turned, wobbled, and finally came to rest.

"Again G? Did you ever see such a winning streak?"

Benny demonstrated his great mastery of the game over and over until he cleaned out all our pockets to the last penny and then thrust his hands in his pockets as if to say, "Well, who's next?"

Slowly, we all drifted home, carrying away with us not only the heartache and shame of losing but the necessity of having to concoct lies to explain where our Chanukah money had gone. Each of us invented a different story. One blurted out that he had spent it all on sweets and carob. Another made up the alibi that someone had robbed him during the night. A third came home crying.

"What is it? Why are you crying?"

"I bought a penknife with my Chanukah money."

"So why are you crying?"

"I lost it on the way home."

I too had to come up with a good story, telling my mother a tale right out of the "Thousand and One Nights." I did succeed in getting her to give me more Chanukah money, which I immediately took over to Benny's, where, within five minutes, I was cleaned out again. Back I went to my mother with still another tall tale. In short, brains were busy, minds were working overtime turning out lies and more lies that flew like woodchips. All our Chanukah money wound up in Benny's pocket, gone forever!

But only one of us became so caught up in the dreydl game

that he didn't stop at just losing his Chanukah money. He gambled and played dreydl with Benny every day until the last day of Chanukah. That person was none other than myself, "the widow's boy."

Where did "the widow's boy" get money with which to gamble? Don't ask. The greatest gamblers in the world, those who have won and lost great fortunes and rich estates, they would know, they would understand. Ah, me! When the desire to gamble takes hold of him, there is no obstacle that a gambler cannot overcome. He will break through brick walls and iron gates, commit unimaginable crimes. That's what the evil gambling habit will make him do.

First of all, I obtained money by selling everything I owned, one article after another, to my eternal shame. First my penknife, then my wallet, and finally, all my buttons. I had a little box which could open and shut and several gears from an old clock made of fine brass which, when polished, shone like real gold. Everything I owned was practically given away at half-price or for whatever I could get, and off I would run with the money to Benny's place to lose it all. I would leave him, my heart wounded, bitterly disappointed, and very angry. But God forbid, not at Benny! Why should I blame Benny? How was Benny responsible for his good luck? He would console me by saying that if I spun the dreydl and it fell on the *G* for me, then I would be the winner; but he was spinning it and it fell on the *G* for him, so naturally, *he* was the winner. That's what Benny said and who could deny it? No, my only disappointment was with myself because I had squandered so much money, my poor mother's hard-earned money as well as my prize possessions, leaving me naked, so to speak, as the day I was born. Even my little Siddur, my daily prayer book, was sold. Oh, that Siddur, that lovely little prayer book! Whenever I remind myself of that little Siddur, my heart aches and my face burns with shame. It was really a treasure, a gem, not a prayer book. It was bought for me by my mother on my father's yahrtzeit, the anniversary of his death, from Petchaya the peddler.

It was a prayer book above and beyond all other prayer books, more like an encyclopedia than a prayer book. It was thick and

packed full of information about anything you could ever dream
of wanting to know: the Song of Songs, commentaries, Sayings
of the Fathers, the Haggadah, all the prayers, laws, and customs
for every day of the year and all the holidays, plus a Book of
Psalms at the back. Not to mention the binding, the gold letter-
ing, and the bold, clear print. An enchantment, I tell you, a
spirit, not a prayer book!

Petchaya the peddler was a man who suffered from cataracts.
His moustache somehow seemed to make his sad face appear
smiling. Whenever Petchaya came around and displayed his
wares at the door of the synagogue, I could not take my eyes off
that little "encyclopedia."

"What are you looking at, young man?" Petchaya would ask
innocently, pretending he didn't know of my desire for the
Siddur even though I had leafed through it seventeen times,
each time asking how much it cost.

"Nothing," I said, "just looking," and I turned away and left
quickly so as not to reveal my passion for it.

"Oh, Momma, you should see what a beautiful little Siddur
Petchaya has!"

"What kind of a Siddur?" asked my mother.

"Such a Siddur! If I had such a Siddur, I would—I would—"

"Don't you have a Siddur already? What about your father's
Siddur?"

"How can you compare them, Momma? That one is just a
Siddur, but *this* one is a regular encyclopedia!"

"An encyclopedia!" my mother exclaimed. "Are there more
prayers in it? Do the prayers sound better?"

Go explain to a mother what an encyclopedia is, a *real*
encyclopedia with red covers, with blue print, and with a green
binding.

"Come," my mother said to me one evening, taking me by the
hand. "Come with me to shul. Tomorrow is your father's
yahrtzeit, so we'll light a candle and on the way home, we'll go
past Petchaya's and see what's so great about that little Siddur."

I knew beforehand that on my father's yahrtzeit I could get
whatever I wanted from my mother, and my heart was already
thumping with anticipation.

Outside the synagogue we found Petchaya with his sack of merchandise still unpacked. Petchaya, you understand, was a man who could not be rushed. He knew full well he had no competition. No one would take any of his business away. It took forever till he untied his pack. I trembled, I shook, I shivered, barely able to stand on my feet while he took his time, as if my nervousness had nothing whatsoever to do with him.

"Show us already," my mother urged him impatiently. "Let's see what kind of a prayer book you have there."

Petchaya had all the time in the world. Where was the fire? Slowly, without hurrying, he untied the sack and spread out his entire merchandise: large and small Bibles, prayer books for men and women, large and small psalm books, holiday prayer books without end, story books, Chassidic tales, and on and on. It seemed to me his supply of books would never end. His sack was bottomless. Finally the smaller items emerged, and among them, my special little Siddur shone forth!

"This is it?" my mother wondered out loud. "Such a little thing?"

"That little thing," said Petchaya, "is more expensive than a big thing."

"How much are you asking—may God forgive my language— for that little pipsqueak?"

"You're calling a prayer book a pipsqueak?" Petchaya was shocked. He slowly removed the book from her hands and my heart sank.

"Well, tell me already, how much does it cost?" my mother relented. But Petchaya had plenty of time and answered in a singsong, "How much does it cost? It costs, it costs! I'm afraid it's out of your range."

My mother cursed her enemies with nightmares and demanded a price. Petchaya quoted a price and my mother remained silent. She turned her face to the door, grabbed my hand, and said to me, "Come, let's go. We have no more business here. Don't you know Reb Petchaya carries only overpriced merchandise?"

With a heavy heart, I followed my mother to the door, hoping against hope that God would have pity on me and Petchaya would call us back. But that's not the kind of man Petchaya was.

He knew we would turn back of our own accord; and that's what happened. We did turn back and my mother pleaded with him to be more reasonable. Petchaya didn't move a muscle, looked up at the ceiling, the white cataract of his left eye glistening, and we walked away and turned back still another time.

"A strange man, that Petchaya!" my mother said to me afterward. "I would rather die of the plague than buy a prayer book from him! It's overpriced. It's shameful. The money could well be used for your tuition, but never mind. In honor of your dear, dead father's yahrtzeit, may he rest in peace, and because tomorrow you will say Kaddish for him, I gave in and bought it for you as a special favor. So you too must do me a favor, my son, and promise me that you'll pray every day faithfully."

Whether or not I actually did pray every day faithfully—well, let's not talk about it. But I adored that little Siddur more than life itself. You can appreciate just how much when I say that I even slept with it, although that's forbidden. The whole cheder envied me my little Siddur, and I guarded it as one would the pupil of an eye. And then, that Chanukah—may God forgive me—with my own hands I delivered it to Moishe, the carpenter's son. He had been dying to get hold of it for some time, but it was I who had to beg *him*, on bended knee, to buy it from me. I gave that little Siddur away for almost nothing! Oh, that little treasure, my very own favorite prayer book! When I think of that little book, I want to cry my heart out and bury my face in my hands with shame. Sold! Traded away, and for what? For whom? For Benny. So that Benny could win a few more pennies from me. But how was it Benny's fault if he had all the luck with the dreydl?

"That's the way dreydls are," Benny said, trying to comfort me as he put away my last few pennies in his pocket. "If you had been the lucky one, you would have won, but I was the lucky one, so I won."

Benny's cheeks were fiery red. His house was bright and cheery. They had a silver Chanukah menorah full of the finest oil with a large shamesh ready to kindle the other wicks. Nothing but the best. From the kitchen one could smell the heavenly aroma of freshly rendered goose fat.

"We're having latkes tonight," Benny told me as we stood at the door, and my stomach rumbled with hunger. I ran home in my torn coat to find my mother just returning from work, her nose and hands red and swollen, frozen through and through, standing at the oven trying to warm herself. Seeing me, her face lit up.

"Coming from shul?" she asked.

"From shul," I lied.

"Said your evening prayers?"

"Said them," I lied again.

"Warm yourself, my son, and you'll say the blessing on the Chanukah candles. Tonight, thank God, we light the last candle."

If a person experienced only suffering, without a moment's pleasure, without a bit of joy, he would be unable to bear it and would surely take his own life. I'm thinking of my mother, that poor widow, who struggled day and night, worked, froze, starved, and went without sleep and for my sake alone, only for me. So why wasn't she entitled to some happiness once in a while? Each person understands the word *happiness* in his own way. For my mother there was no greater happiness than my chanting the kiddush for her on Sabbath and holidays, my conducting the seder for her at Passover, or my blessing the candles for her at Chanukah. What did it matter whether we used real wine or not on the Sabbath, what did it matter whether we enjoyed special Passover pastries or just stale matzos softened with water for Passover, what did it matter whether we had a silver menorah or used scooped-out potato halves filled with oil for Chanukah? Believe me, neither the wine nor the pastries nor the silver were what really counted. What really counted was something else. It was the actual performance of the kiddush, the celebration of the seder, and the blessing of the Chanukah candles. She didn't have to tell me how she was feeling or explain to me why; her face, smiling and glowing with pride as I chanted the blessing, said it all. Then one could appreciate that *this* was real happiness, *this* was true good fortune.

I bowed my head over the scooped-out potato halves and chanted the blessing and she chanted after me under her breath, word for word with the same melody. I prayed and she looked directly into my eyes as she moved her lips and I knew what was going on in her heart. She was thinking, "Altogether 'him,' his very image. May his years be many." I felt that all I deserved was to be cut up like those scooped-out potatoes. After all, I had deceived my mother and in such an ugly way! I sold my little Siddur and lost the money gambling with the dreydl! I sold it, I gave away my very soul!

The wicks in the potatoes, our Chanukah candles, smoked and sputtered and were finally extinguished. My mother said to me, "Go wash up and we'll eat potatoes with goose fat. In honor of Chanukah, I splurged and bought a jar of goose fat—fresh, delicious goose fat." I washed up happily and we sat down at the table to eat.

"Those who are well off can afford to have latkes the last day of Chanukah," my mother said with a deep sigh, and I thought of Benny's latkes and Benny's dreydl which had cost me such a fortune and my heart felt as if it had been pierced with a needle.

Even during the night my thoughts would not let me alone. I could hear my mother's constant moaning and the creaking of her bed as she tossed and turned. I imagined that the bed too was moaning, not creaking. Outside, the wind howled, rattled the windows, tore at the roof, and whistled in the chimney with a long, drawn-out *pheeeww!* A cricket, nesting in the walls since summer, chirped from its hiding place, "Chireree-chireree!" and my mother didn't stop moaning. Every moan and every sigh reverberated in my heart until I could barely control myself. I was on the verge of leaping from my bed and running to my mother's side, falling on my knees, kissing her hands, and confessing all my terrible sins. But I didn't do it. Instead I drew my blankets over my head so as not to hear my mother's bed creaking and her moaning and sighing.

I shut my eyes tight, the wind whistled and howled—*pheeeww!*—and the cricket chirped, "Chireree-chireree! Chireree-chireree!" and suddenly there seemed to be something spinning before my eyes, something like a dreydl shaped like a person, a familiar person. I could have sworn it was the rebbi with his pointy yarmulke. The rebbi was standing on one leg, Bible in hand, spinning, spinning, spinning like a dreydl, his pointy yarmulke shimmering on his head, his earlocks swirling in the air. No, it wasn't the rebbi but really a dreydl! A strange dreydl, a live dreydl with a pointy yarmulke and flying earlocks. Gradually, gradually, the rebbi-like dreydl or the dreydl-like rebbi stopped spinning and in its place there materialized Pharaoh, the King of Egypt, about whom we had just studied in cheder the week before Chanukah. Pharaoh, the King of Egypt, stood before my eyes stark naked, having just emerged from the pond, and in his hand was my little Siddur, my little encyclopedia, and I couldn't figure out how it had fallen into the hands of this wicked monster who had bathed in Jewish blood.

Then I saw seven cows—thin, haggard, emaciated, nothing but skin and bone with enormous horns and long ears, coming at me all at the same time, their mouths wide open, about to swallow me. Suddenly, there was Benny, my friend Benny. He grabbed the cattle by their long ears and gave them each a good twist while someone wept softly, sighed and sobbed, moaned and whistled and chirped. A figure was standing beside my bed, speaking quietly, gently, "Tell me, my son, when is my yahrtzeit? When will you say Kaddish for me?"

I saw that it was my father from the beyond, my father about whom my mother had told me all those wonderful things. I wanted to tell him when his yahrtzeit was, when I would say Kaddish for him—but I forgot! Just then I forgot! I struggled to remember, rubbed my forehead, tried to remind myself—but I couldn't! Have you ever heard anything like it? I forgot when my own father's yahrtzeit was! Help! Help! Help!

"God be with you! Why are you screaming? What's this yelling about? Does anything hurt you, God forbid?"

My mother was bending over me, holding my head, and I could feel her body trembling and shaking. The dim little bedside lamp was smoking, shedding little light, and I could see my mother's shadow dancing crazily on the wall, the points of her kerchief looking like two horns. Her eyes glinted frighteningly in the dark.

"When is Poppa's yahrtzeit? Tell me, Momma! When is Poppa's yahrtzeit?"

"God help you! It was just not long ago. Did you have a bad dream? Spit three times—Tfu! Tfu! Tfu! May all be for the best. Amen! Amen! Amen!"

I grew up and became an adult. Benny also grew up and became an adult, a young man with a yellow beard. He acquired a little paunch on which he sported a gold chain. Obviously, he was well-to-do, Benny. Once he was a rich man's son, now he was a rich man himself.

We met on a train. I recognized him by his bulging fish-eyes and widely spaced teeth. It had been a long time since we had seen one another. We embraced and were soon reminiscing about the dear old bygone days of our childhood, reminding ourselves of all the foolish deeds we had done.

"Remember, Benny, that Chanukah when you were so lucky at dreydl? Your dreydl kept falling on the *G!*"

I looked at my friend, Benny. He was breaking up with laughter. He held his sides, doubled over, almost choking to death with laughter.

"God help you, Benny! Why this sudden laughter?"

"Oh!" He gesticulated with both hands. "Don't talk about that dreydl! That was *some* dreydl! *Really* a dreydl! That was a pot of gold, pure gold! With such a dreydl it was hard to lose. Whichever side it fell on, it had to fall on the—ha ha ha—on the *G!*"

"What kind of a dreydl was *that*, Benny?"

"That was—ha ha ha—a dreydl with nothing but *G*'s. Pure *G!* A *G* on every side, ha ha ha!"

A Ruined Passover

"REB Yisroel! Reb Yisroel? Please. I must know! Can you promise me to have the boy's suit ready for the holidays?"

So shouted my mother to Yisroel the tailor at the top of her lungs because Yisroel the tailor was almost stone deaf. A tall Jew with a long face and with cotton stuffed in his ears, Yisroel smiled half to himself and gestured with his hand as if to say, "Why shouldn't it be ready?"

"So, please, take his measurements, but only on the condition that you'll have it ready for Passover."

Yisroel the deaf tailor looked at my mother as if to say, "What a strange woman! Doesn't she think I heard her the first time?"

He pulled out a long tape measure from his vest pocket, stood me in front of him, and started to measure me in the length and in the width as my mother stood alongside, carrying on: "Longer, much longer! Wider, much wider! Don't make the trousers too narrow! Make sure the jacket has an extra fold in it—at least several inches so it can be let out next year. Wider! More, a little wider! That's the way! Whatever you do, don't make the waist too short, God forbid! Nicely now, with style! More, more! Don't scrimp on cloth, because a child grows!"

Yisroel the tailor knew very well that "a child grows" and went right on about his business. Having measured my arms and legs, he dismissed me with a slight shove as if to say, "You can go now. You're free!" I very much wanted the jacket to have a split and a pocket in the back, which was then in style, but I didn't know whom to ask. Yisroel the deaf tailor wound his tape measure on two fingers as he talked to my mother in fragmented phrases: "A busy time before Passover! . . . Mud—there's plenty! . . . Fish—scarce! . . . Potatoes—expensive! . . . Eggs—not to be found! . . .

Work—forget it! . . . New clothes—not a chance! . . . Just patchwork, patchwork, patchwork! . . . Even Reb Yehoshua Hersh can
only afford to have an old coat turned inside out—imagine! . . .
Reb Yehoshua Hersh himself! . . . Such a time—the world is
coming to an end!"

My mother wasn't impressed. She interrupted him in the
middle of his ramblings. "About how much do you think it will
come to, Reb Yisroel?"

Yisroel the deaf tailor removed a snuffbox made of horn from
his vest pocket, cupped his hand and shook out a little mound of
snuff into it, drew it slowly to his nose, and inhaled the snuff so
deftly that not even a speck fell on his moustache. Then he gestured with his hand and said, "What does it matter? We won't
argue about it. . . . Did you ever hear such a thing? Reb Yehoshua
Hersh! . . . Turning an old coat inside out! . . . God in heaven!"

"Remember now, Reb Yisroel, what I'm asking—not too
tight, not too short, with an extra fold and the waist—roomy
and full."

"And with a split . . . ?" I started to add.

"Be quiet, we're talking!" scolded my mother and jabbed me
in the ribs with her elbow. And to Yisroel, "I'll remind you
again—not too short, not too tight, with an extra fold and the
waist—roomy and full."

"And with a pocket . . . ?" I tried again.

"You won't be still, will you?" my mother warned. "Did you
ever see such a child who keeps interrupting while grownups
are talking?"

Yisroel the deaf tailor tucked the package of cloth under his
arm, passed two fingers across the mezuzah on the doorpost, and
called from the doorway, "Does that mean you really want it to
be ready for Passover? Happy holiday to you! Goot yom-tov!"

"Ah, here's Reb Gedalyeh! Speak of the devil! I was just thinking of sending for you again."

Gedalyeh was a shoemaker, an old soldier who had served his
time, whose front teeth were missing and whose large, round
beard had obviously once been shaven in the middle, where
now straggly hairs grew.

"Reb Gedalyeh," my mother said to him, "tell me, can you promise to make a pair of shoes for my son for Passover?"

Gedalyeh the shoemaker was a cheerful Jew who accompanied whatever he said with a sideways hop. "Oh, you want them ready for Passover!" he said, almost sarcastically, to my mother. "What a surprise! Just about everyone else wants them ready for Passover too. I promised Chaya, Reb Mottel's daughter, two pairs of boots, one pair for her and one for her daughter, so I have that to do. Yossele, Reb Shemele's son, ordered four pairs of shoes for Passover, so I have to make them for him. I promised to make Feigele, Reb Abraham's daughter, a pair of boots a long time ago. Even if the sky were to fall, I'd have to make *them!* And Moishe the tailor asked me to repair his heels and I can't turn him down. Zyma the carpenter needs new soles, which doesn't help my situation. Just today, Asna the widow's girl was pestering me to——"

"So!" my mother cut him short. "Let's be perfectly frank. Does that mean you won't be able to have them ready for Passover? Because if not, I'll call another shoemaker . . ."

"Why shouldn't I be able to?" said Gedalyeh with a little hop. "Just for you, I'll set aside my other work and you'll definitely have your shoes for Passover. Is there any reason not to?"

And Gedalyeh the shoemaker took out a piece of blue paper, got down on one knee, and began tracing my foot.

"Add a few more inches!" ordered my mother. "More, more! Why are you so stingy with the leather? That's the way! We don't want it to pinch his toes!"

"Pinch his toes . . ." Gedalyeh repeated my mother's last words.

"Be sure it's good leather, not second grade!"

"Second grade . . ." Gedalyeh repeated.

"Put on good soles so they won't wear out!"

"Wear out . . ." Gedalyeh echoed.

"And the heels shouldn't come off!"

"Come off . . ."

"Now you can go to cheder," my mother said to me. "Do you see how much trouble we go to for your sake? If you would only want to study, you could become somebody. Otherwise, what will become of you? You'll be a nobody, a nothing, a dogcatcher!"

I myself didn't know what would become of me—a somebody, a nobody, or a dogcatcher. I only knew that more than anything else in the world, I wanted shoes that would squeak. Oh, how I wanted real squeakers!

"Why are you standing there like a lamppost?" my mother called out to me. "Why don't you go to cheder? Go, that's all the clothing you're going to get."

Gedalyeh the shoemaker started to leave but turned around. "That means you really want them ready for Passover?" he said. "Well, happy holiday! Goot yom-tov!"

On the way home from cheder that day, I ducked into the tailor's shop to see about the split and the pocket for my new jacket. There at a large table stood Yisroel the deaf tailor without his jacket, revealing the short fringed ritual garment men wore under their clothing. He was absorbed in his work; several long threads hung around his neck and a few needles were stuck into his vest. He was marking something with chalk, then cutting the material with a large pair of English scissors while scratching his back with a bent middle finger and mumbling to himself in his absent-minded way, "Extra folds they want . . . it should be roomy . . . make it wide. . . . With what? . . . out of thin air? . . . You slice your fingers . . . you struggle . . . struggle. . . . Like they were boiled meat . . ."

Around the table sat several young apprentice tailors sewing, their needles flying as they sang a song in unison. One of them, a freckle-faced, blond youngster with a flattened nose, sang in a strident voice, drawing his needle in time to the music:

> Oh, ain't you leavin',
> And oh, ain't you leavin' me,
> Ain't you leavin' me far be-ee-hind!

The others joined him with a shrill,

> I'm gonna stab myself!
> I'm gonna hang myself!
> I'm gonna drown myself!
> I'm gonna do myself i-in!

"What's on your mind, young man?" Yisroel motioned to me. "A split," I ventured.

"A what?" Yisroel bent over closer to me, cupping his ear.

"A split!" I shouted out loud so he could hear.

"A split?"

"A split!"

"Where do you want a split?"

"In the back!"

"What do you want in the back?"

"A split! And a pocket!"

"What split? What pocket?" interjected Batyeh, the tailor's wife, a small woman who sat and did three jobs at once: with her foot she rocked the baby's cradle, with her hands she knitted a sock, and with her mouth she argued and complained. "Why do you need a split? Why do you need a pocket? Where do you have cloth for a pocket? He wants pockets? Let his mother give him cloth for pockets, then he'll have pockets! How about that, pockets!"

I was beginning to regret the whole thing. What if my mother were to find out about it?

"So you really want a split, eh?" Yisroel the tailor asked, taking out his snuffbox. "Go home, young man, you'll have your split."

"And a pocket too?" I said to him, putting on a sad face.

"Go home, young man," Yisroel said again. "I'll see to it that it's just the way you want it."

Joyfully, I ran off to Gedalyeh the shoemaker to arrange for the squeaks in my shoes. Gedalyeh the shoemaker was out. At a bench sat his worker, Karpa, flattening out a large piece of leather. Karpa was a healthy, broad-boned peasant with a pimply face who wore a leather visor over his coarse, black hair.

"What do you want, boy?" Karpa tried to say in Yiddish as best as he could. "Speak! What you want?"

He knew a few common Yiddish words and proceeded to rattle them off for my benefit, "Shmata, shlemiel, chutzpah, goniff."

"I would like to talk to your boss, Reb Gedalyeh," I answered in my best Russian.

"Boss go to circumcision," Karpa tried again in Yiddish. "Make kiddush, drink branfy." In order to make sure I understood what he meant, he drew his finger across his throat.

I sat down opposite him on a leather stool and engaged him in a discussion about leather, about heels and soles, about staining and so on, until finally we came around to discussing squeaks. He talked in Yiddish, I in Russian. He couldn't understand everything I was saying, so I used my hands to help.

"I'm talking to you in your own language, fathead," I said in Yiddish, and then in Russian, "Tell me, how do you make shoes squeak? You know, *trrr! trrr!*"

"You better talk Yiddish," said Karpa and licked the leather with his tongue, then made a deep mark on the side of it with his thick, black fingernail.

"How come shoes squeak?" I now spoke in Yiddish. "What's the trick in getting squeaks? What do you put in shoes to make them squeak?"

"Ah, squeaks?" said Karpa. "For to make squeaks you need sugar cube."

"Just a sugar cube?" I wondered. "How come?"

"Sugar cube," Karpa explained. "Sugar—pound-pound, squeak-squeak . . ."

"Aha!" I nodded. "You probably pound the sugar into a powder and that makes them squeak. Well, and don't you add anything else?"

"Some branfy," Karpa said, mispronouncing the word again. "A little branfy."

"Brandy?" I wondered. "You mean vodka? Why vodka? Sugar I can understand; squeak-squeak! But *vodka?* How does that help make them squeak?"

Karpa made a great effort to tell me in Yiddish so I could understand how the vodka would do the job. "Before you put sugar on soles, you wet with branfy so sugar stick."

"Aha!" I exclaimed. "Now I get it! If there's no vodka, the sugar won't work, and without the sugar, the shoes won't squeak. As it says in the Bible, 'Without food, there is no Torah.'" I opened my wallet and gave Karpa everything I had left from my Chanukah and Purim money. We parted on friendly terms as Karpa shoved his big, glue-stained hand in mine. I hurried home for lunch and from there, sped back to cheder where I bragged to all my friends about the fine clothing that was being made for me for Passover—a jacket with a split and a pocket in the back and shoes that squeaked! Squeaked! Squeaked!

✿   ✿   ✿

"Momma, no more school!" I ran into the house a few days before Passover proclaiming the great news to my mother that we had been let out of school early.

"Just what I needed! May you live to bring home better news!" my mother scowled, all caught up with preparations for Passover. She and both servant girls had tied white kerchiefs on their heads and, armed with brushes and feather dusters, the three of them were busily cleaning and mopping, scrubbing and scouring, waxing and polishing, getting the house clean and kosher for Passover. Nothing, not a speck of food, not an item of clothing, not a single eating utensil used during the year could be allowed in the house for Passover. All those things were *chometz*. I couldn't find a spot for myself without being told to move. Wherever I sat and wherever I went—no good!

"Get away from the clean Passover cupboard with that *chometz* clothing!" my mother screamed at me with such alarm you would have thought I had lit a match near gunpowder. "Careful, you're stepping on a Passover sack!" and "Don't you even dare to *look* over there, at that Passover borscht!"

I wandered from one place to the next, always underfoot; a shove, a smack, or a pinch always awaited me. "What came over that rebbi of yours? Couldn't he keep you in cheder another day? As if we didn't have enough work to do, who needs you hanging around? Some people's children sit in one place like they're supposed to. Isn't there something better a boy your age can do with himself? Why don't you go over the Four Questions?"

"But Momma," I said, "I already know them by heart."

"So?" said my mother. "Would it hurt to go over them again?"

At last evening came; it wasn't easy, but I made it. My father went around the house with a candle, a wooden spoon, and a feather duster searching out the last of the bread. I helped him find the bread crumbs which he himself had placed on the window sills as part of the ritual.

"Only twenty-four hours to go!" I thought. "Only one more night and one more day and then I'll be able to get all dressed up for Passover like a prince, in a new jacket with a split and a pocket in the back, and shoes that will squeak as I walk. I'll bet

Momma will ask, 'What's all that squeaking?' and I'll pretend I don't know what she's talking about. And what about the seder, the Four Questions, the four glasses of wine, and all the Passover treats: latkes, dumplings, pastries . . ." Just thinking about these dishes made my mouth water. I had hardly eaten a thing all day.

"Finish up your evening prayers," my mother said, "and go to bed. There's no supper tonight; it's the night before Passover."

I went to sleep and dreamed it was already Passover. I was going to shul with my father. My new clothes were crackling, my new shoes were squeaking—Squeak! Squeak! Squeak! "Who is *that?*" strangers wanted to know. "That's Mottel, Moishe-Chayim Avraham-Hersh Reuven's son." Suddenly, from out of nowhere, a black, shaggy dog leaped up at me—"Bow-wow!"—and grabbed hold of my jacket with his teeth. My father, afraid to come near, tried to chase the dog away by making threatening gestures with his hands and shouting, "Scat! Scat!" The dog didn't obey him and continued to tear at my coat from behind, right where the split and the pocket were, ripping off half the jacket and starting to run away with it. I ran after him with all my might but lost a shoe. I was left stuck in the mud with one shoe on and one bare foot. I started to cry and scream, "Help! Help! Help!"

I awoke with a start and saw our servant girl, Bayla, standing near me, yanking my blanket off and tugging at my leg.

"It's impossible to wake him up! Come on, get up! Your mother told me to get you up. You have to help carry out the last of the *chometz*."

My father tossed the wooden spoon, the feather duster, and the last of the *chometz* into the oven. The house was officially ready for Passover—clean everywhere, kosher everywhere, the table set, the wine glasses winking at me from across the room. Soon, soon, in an hour, in just one hour, I would be getting dressed for the holiday. But until the tailor and the shoemaker came with my Passover outfit, my mother found time to get me ready for the holiday in her own way. She shampooed my hair with hot, soapy water in which she had dissolved an egg yolk.

She combed my hair, yanking it hard. If I so much as cringed, she would jab me with her elbow or slap me. "Stop wriggling like a worm, hear? Did you ever see such a child who can't stand still? You do nice things for him and he still isn't satisfied!"

I survived the shampoo, thank God, and sat at the table in my shirt waiting for my new outfit to arrive. I looked over at my father, who had just come back from the bathhouse, his earlocks still damp. He was sitting bent over a thick book silently studying a portion from the Gemorah, humming and swaying gently.

As I looked at my father, I imagined that nowhere in the world was there a man as virtuous as he, that nowhere in the world was there a more perfect Passover than ours, and nowhere in the world could clothes like mine be found. But why weren't they here yet? What was the delay? What if they weren't ready in time for the beginning of Passover? I refused to even *think* of that! How would I go to shul? What would my friends say? How would I sit at the seder table? God forbid! I'd never live it down!

As I sat considering these grim possibilities, the door opened and in came Yisroel the tailor with my suit. Thrilled to see him, I sprang up excitedly and fell over together with my chair, almost breaking my neck. My mother ran in from the kitchen with a Passover ladle in her hand. "What was that loud noise? Who fell down? Who? It's *you*, is it? May the devil take you, God forbid! A demon! An imp! Did you hurt yourself, God protect you? Serves you right! Don't run! Don't jump! Walk the way you're supposed to!" And to Yisroel she said, "You kept your word, Reb Yisroel—I was about to send for you."

Yisrel gave a half-smile and waved his hand, as if to say, "What did you expect? Did you think I wouldn't keep my word?"

My mother put down the ladle and helped me into the new trousers and then put on the fringed undergarment that she herself had sewn for Passover. On top of that she put on the jacket and seemed content that it was roomy and wide enough.

Immediately, I felt around behind me in the back of the coat. Oh! Oh! Big problems! A disaster! Not a sign of a split or a pocket! Sewn up, smooth and even, all around!

"What's this bunched-up sausage here?" my mother suddenly wanted to know as she turned me around.

Yisroel took out his snuffbox, cupped his hand, poured in a little mound of snuff, and inhaled it quickly.

"What's this bunched-up sausage here?" my mother repeated more loudly and turned me around the other way.

"That's the extra fold you ordered. Did you forget already?"

"That's some fold!" said my mother, giving me another turn. "It's an awful mess, shameful! Shameful! A disgrace, absolutely a disgrace!"

Yisroel's pride was, I assure you, not injured. He studied me carefully from head to toe like a professor and said that it fit extraordinarily well, couldn't be better. "Such workmanship can't be found even in Paris. The jacket *sings,* as I am a Jew, it actually *sings!*"

"This kind of singing appeals to you?" said my mother and led me over to my father. "What do you say to this song?"

My father turned me around and around, examined the suit, and allowed as how the trousers were indeed a bit too long. Yisroel removed the snuffbox again and honored my father with a sniff.

"Reb Yisroel, don't you think perhaps the pants are on the long side?"

"Ha? What? On the long side, you say? Don't you know what to do? You roll them up!"

"Maybe you're right," said my father. "But what do we do about the width? The legs look like two sacks."

"Some complaint! That's like saying the bride is too beautiful," said Yisroel and took another sniff. "Too wide, did you say? Narrow is worse, a thousand times worse!"

I couldn't stop feeling around the back of the coat, searching in vain for a split or a pocket.

"What are you looking for back there?" my mother said. "Where yesterday went?"

"You swindler!" I thought to myself, looking at Yisroel with hatred. "You rotten, lying, deaf old swindler!"

"Wear it in good health!" Yisroel the deaf tailor said to me after he had settled his account. My father returned to his studies, resuming the same chanting.

"Wear it well!" my mother said to me after Yisroel the tailor had left. She couldn't stop admiring my jacket. "If only you don't start up with any bullies or get into any fights with the peasant boys, you'll be able to wear that suit forever, may you live and be well."

"Well, well, here's Reb Gedalyeh!" said my mother. "Speaking of the devil! Are the boy's shoes ready?"

"What do you mean? Of course they're ready!" said Gedalyeh the shoemaker with a little dance step, holding the polished shoes on his two fingers as one would hold two freshly caught fish. "It's unbelievable! The whole world wants shoes ready for Passover. I worked my fingers to the bone, didn't sleep a wink! Me, when I give my word, neither thunder nor lightning can stop me."

My mother helped me on with my shoes, then pinched and squeezed my feet and asked me if they were, heaven forbid, too tight.

"Too tight?" said Gedalyeh. "It seems to me that you can put another pair of feet in those shoes!"

"Here, stand up!" said my mother. I stood up and pressed down on the soles, hoping to hear them squeak. What! Not a sound out of them!

"Why are you pressing down so hard?" asked my mother. "Don't worry, they're big enough for now, but I guarantee you'll wear them out before Passover, may we live and be well, if you keep pushing down on them. Now go with your father to Yechiel the hatter and he'll pick out a nice holiday hat for you. But be careful with the shoes! Don't stomp so hard on the soles! They're not made of iron!"

Yechiel the hatter's shop was near our house, right across the courtyard. Yechiel, as luck would have it, was born pale and fair with very light blond hair, but since he always handled black-dyed hats, he was constantly stained. His nose was almost completely blue and his fingers looked as if they had been dipped in ink.

"Welcome, neighbor, come in!" Yechiel the hatter said to us cheerfully. "Who's the holiday hat for? For you or your son?"

"For my son," my father replied proudly. "I want you to show me something really nice . . . something special . . . you know what I mean? . . ."

"I just happen to have exactly what you want," said Yechiel and took several hats off the shelf, making one twirl around on his finger as he removed it. One after another, he tried the hats on me, stepped back, looked at my face smilingly, and said to my father, "May this year be as blessed as this hat fits him! Well? How do you like that one? That's *really* a hat!"

"No, Reb Yechiel, that's not what I meant," said my father as he scanned the shelves. "I was thinking of a hat that would be . . . *you* know, more 'Jewish' . . . but stylish . . . without any frills . . . well made . . . and . . . and . . . and . . . do you know what I mean?"

"Why didn't you say so?" said Yechiel, and with a long pole, he quickly removed from the top shelf an oval-shaped hat with a colorfully checkered design and a soft brim. He carried it on one finger, spinning it around quickly like a windmill. Then, carefully, he set it on the top of my head so that it barely touched, as if my head were made of spun glass and he was afraid of shattering it. He wished that the year to come would be as suitable to him as this hat was for me. He had, he swore, just one hat like this left. My father bargained with him and Yechiel protested that only to us would he give the hat away so cheaply, almost below cost, may he have a kosher Passover and a healthy life.

I could tell that the hat really pleased my father because he kept coming over to me, admiring it, and smoothing down my earlocks.

"I hope it lasts a summer," said my father.

"Two summers!" cried Yechiel, hopping over to my father. "Three summers! May I live and be well, that's a fine hat! Wear it in good health!"

By the time I reached home, the hat was already down over my ears. I was beginning to suspect that it was a bit large for me.

"Don't fret. So long as it isn't tight," said my mother, pulling the hat down to my nose. "Just don't keep taking it on and off every minute! Don't touch it with your hands! Wear it in good health!"

All my friends were already at shul that evening when my father and I arrived. There stood Itzik and Berel, Leibel and Isaac, Tzadduk and Velvel, Shmaya and Koppel, Mayer and Chayim Sholem, Schachneh and Shepsel, and more and more. All were dressed up in their holiday outfits, all with new jackets, all with new shoes and new hats. But no one wore as long a jacket with a "fold" as mine, no one wore shoes as huge as mine, and I didn't see anyone with a hat as strange as mine. And as for a split, a pocket, squeaky shoes—not at all! I had really been taken in, deceived!

The boys greeted me with laughter. "*Those* are the new clothes you were bragging about? Where's the split in the back? Where's the pocket you said you'd have? How come we don't hear your shoes squeaking?"

I was suffering enough as it was, but they really rubbed salt in the wounds. Each boy humiliated me with his own clever remark:

Itzik said: "What kind of a quilt is that?"

Berel: "A horse blanket!"

Leibel: "A coarse blanket!"

Isaac: "A horse crank-it!"

Tzadduk: "A crock!"

Velvel: "A frock!"

Shmaya: "A petticoat!"

Koppel: "Look at that pair of canal boats!"

Mayer: "And that bat for a hat!"

Chayim Sholem: "A pot for a hat!"

Shachneh: "A noodle bowl!"

Shepsel: "A garbage pail!"

I was so furious that I didn't even hear how beautifully Hersh-Ber the cantor was chanting. I didn't calm down until the congregation was wishing one another, "Happy holiday! Goot yom-tov!" With a heavy heart, I went home with my father, barely able to drag my feet. I felt as if my insides were on fire. I was in no mood to enjoy the four glasses of wine we would soon be drinking, the Four Questions I would soon be asking my father, the Haggadah we would soon be reciting, the delicious peppered fish we would be eating, dipping our matzos in the sauce, the hot dumplings, the Passover pastries and the latkes along with all the other marvelous dishes. Everything, everything seemed so unappealing, dull, ruined, utterly ruined!

At the head of the seder table sat my father, the king, wearing his white linen robe and his velvet Passover hat. He was leaning comfortably on his pile of pillows. Beside him sat my mother, the queen, in her old-fashioned dress, wearing her silk kerchief and the fine pearls which so enhanced her beauty. I, the prince, sat opposite them, clad entirely in new clothes from head to toe. On one side of me sat Bayla, the servant girl, decked out in her new chintz smock and white starched apron which crackled like a matzo. On my other side sat the cook, Brayna, a woman with whiskers, wearing a new yellow kerchief on her head. She held her head in one hand and swayed back and forth, ready to listen to the reciting of the Haggadah.

"*Keho lachman aniyah*—this bread of affliction," sang the king with a pleasant voice, and the queen helped him raise the matzo platter to show all assembled. Her face was shining and bright as a star. Bayla lowered her red hands to her white apron, which rustled like a leaf. As soon as Brayna the cook heard the first Hebrew word, she put on a pious expression and screwed her face up, ready to cry.

Everyone was in a good mood, in fine holiday spirits, except for the prince who was out of sorts. His heart felt as if it had turned to stone, his eyes were glazed. Were it not Passover night, he would have broken down and cried and perhaps that would have made him feel better.

"*Hashanah avdi*—this year we are slaves," the king sang out with pride. "*L'shanah habah b'nai chorin*—next year we will be free."

The king leaned back on his pile of pillows and everyone else followed suit. They all waited for the prince to rise and ask the Four Questions, which began with "*Ma nishtanah halaylah hazeh*—wherefore is this night different from all other nights of the year?" Then the king would respond by relating the story of Passover: "*Avodim hayinu*—slaves we were . . . ." But the prince remained seated as if welded to his chair. He couldn't move.

"Well?" said the king.

"Stand up," said the queen. "Ask your father the Four Questions."

The prince didn't budge. He felt as if somebody had clamped his throat in a vice and was strangling him. He couldn't hold his head up straight. His eyes felt as if they would pop out of their sockets. Two tears, like two pearls, slipped from his eyes down his cheeks and fell onto the Haggadah.

"What's the matter? Why this sudden crying right in the middle of the seder?" the queen scolded me angrily. "Is this the way you thank us for the new holiday clothes we had made for you?"

The prince wanted to stop crying but couldn't; he was too choked with tears. Suddenly the tears gushed out, as if a floodgate had burst.

"Speak! What's the matter with you? What's hurting you? Why don't you answer? Tell us, or do you want your father to put you across his knee and give you a spanking in honor of Passover?"

The prince stood up, trying with difficulty to pull himself together, and stumbled over his words, "Question, I wish to ask you the Four Fathers . . . I mean, Father, I wish to ask you the Four Ques– Que . . ."

The prince's legs buckled under him and he collapsed with his head on the white tablecloth, sobbing and blubbering like an infant.

"A ruined Passover! A ruined Passover!"

The Esrog

M Y real name is Ori Leib but I've always been called Leibel, and in cheder they nicknamed me "Leib-Dreib-Obderik." In our cheder every boy had a rhyming nickname: Mottel-Kappotel, Mayer-Drayer, Mendel-Fendel, Chayim-Klayim, Itzik-Shpitzik, Berel-Tzop. How do you like that for rhyming? Certainly Itzik goes with Shpitzik, Mendel with Fendel, and Chayim with Klayim—quite understandable; but how does Berel go with Tzop? And how do you figure Leib-Dreib-Obderik? It drove me wild. I would fight over it constantly and get more than my share of pushes, shoves, pokes, jabs, punches, and socks from all sides. I was made black and blue because I was the smallest one in our cheder, the smallest and the weakest and the poorest— a circumstance that counted for little in Kasrilevka. No one ever stood up for me or defended my cause. On the contrary, if two rich boys beat me up, one straddling me like a horse and the other twisting my ear, a third boy, a poor man's son like myself, would stand alongside, egging them on, chanting:

Atta boy! Atta boy!
Give it to him! Give it to him!
Twist 'em off! Twist 'em off!
Atta boy! Atta boy!

I would lie still as a kitten, but when they finally let me up, I would go off into a corner and cry quietly. Then I would dry my eyes, pull myself together, and slip back with the gang, trying to act as if nothing had happened. So, whenever you read the name "Leibel" in this story, know that it's me.

In appearance, I might have struck you as short and chubby,

43

even fat. But really, I wasn't fat. I was actually skinny. I looked fat because I wore heavy quilted cotton trousers, a heavy quilted cotton shirt, and a heavy quilted cotton jacket. My mother wanted to make sure that I was warm and wouldn't catch cold, God forbid, so she wrapped me in quilted cotton from head to toe. But she didn't realize that cotton batting can come in handy. Cotton batting can be wadded into balls, and balls can be thrown. So I distributed cotton batting to all the boys, pulling it out of my trousers and my jacket until my mother noticed it, and then I received even more pushes, shoves, pokes, jabs, punches, and socks. But that didn't stop me. I went on being the supplier of cotton batting to all comers. Whoever wanted helped himself to my cotton batting, and whoever was so inclined beat me to within an inch of my life.

"Leib-Dreib-Obderik! Serves him right! Serves him right!"

But I had something else in mind to tell you. I wanted to tell a story about an esrog but I got carried away who-knows-where.

My father, Moshe Yankel the clerk, had been working in a tax collector's office for as long as anyone could remember. He earned four and a half rubles a week and was looking forward to getting a raise. Once he received his raise, with God's help, he said he would buy an esrog, that special exotic citron so important to the Sukkos ceremony. But my mother, Batya Beile the clerk's wife, as she was called, didn't count on such good luck. "Cows will have kittens," she said, "before a tax collector will give you a raise." Once, before Rosh Hashanah, Leibel overheard this exchange between his parents:

"I don't care if the world turns upside down, but this Sukkos we must have our own esrog!"

"The world won't turn upside down and you won't have an esrog."

"That's what you say. What would you say if I told you I was promised a bonus toward an esrog?"

"That will be the day. It will go into the record books, I'm sure. But if I don't believe it, don't be too surprised."

"I don't care what you believe. I tell you that this Sukkos we are going to have our own esrog."

"Amen, let's hope so. From your mouth into God's ear."

"Amen! Amen! Amen!" Leibel said to himself and already pictured his father going to shul like a respected elder with his own esrog and with his own lulav, the ceremonial bundle of palm, myrtle, and willow branches. Then he could promenade before the Holy Ark like the other wealthy Jews who sat near the eastern wall. Leibel's heart was full of joy and pride. He could picture it in his mind. First, as usual, would come Reb Melech the cantor, like a general, step by step, his head held majestically high, chanting in his pure tenor voice, *"Hosa-na, aniyah soarah, hosa-na!"* Behind him followed the rabbi, a frail, perspiring man, his prayer shawl almost covering his face. After the rabbi, the assistant rabbi, a man with a yellow parchmentlike skin, broad shoulders, and a fat belly which quivered underneath his shiny satin gaberdine. Then came the elders, the rich folks, the cream of the congregation, followed by the merchants, who were in turn followed by the small-businessmen and so on and so forth, one behind the other, a rich man behind a rich man, a merchant behind a merchant, each according to his station, each according to his rank, like an army marching to battle. Leibel could see his father slipping in among the finest merchants, holding his esrog proudly.

After Leibel overheard the conversation between his parents about buying their own esrog, he couldn't keep the news to himself. He let it be known in cheder that this Sukkos his family would have an esrog, their very own esrog. But no one believed him no matter how much he insisted.

"What's going on with his father?" the fellows jeered among themselves. "That pauper, that down-and-out pauper is going to buy his own esrog? I bet he thinks it's a lemon or an apple you can buy for a groshen."

The young ones chanted along:

> Leib-Dreib-Obderik!
> Made up a lie!
> Made up a lie!

And along with the jeering and the chanting, they honored him, as always, with pushes, shoves, pokes, jabs, punches, and socks.

This incident really upset Leibel, as you might expect, and he began to doubt whether his father, a poor man, had the right to desire something beyond his means. Imagine his surprise when he came home and discovered Henzel the shochet wearing his Napoleonic cap, sitting with his father at the table. In front of them stood a basket of esrogs whose presence were made known by their heavenly aroma.

The cap which Henzel the shochet wore was the kind of hat worn in the time of the first Napoleon. In France the hat has long since gone out of style, but to Kasrilevka somehow one such cap had found its way, and it belonged to Henzel the shochet. The cap was long and narrow and had a split in the front, and at the base of the split there was a gold button from which hung two tassels. I was always fascinated by those tassels. If this cap were ever to fall into my hands for so much as two minutes, those tassels would be mine! That was my scheme. But Henzel never removed the cap from his head, and I somehow imagined that the tassels, the cap, Henzel's earlocks, and his head had grown together into one piece because when he spoke and gestured with his hands, his earlocks would shake and the tassels would bounce in unison. Reb Henzel the shochet laid out his wares, selected one esrog, and, holding it carefully between two fingers, brought it over to my father, indicating that this was the one for him.

"Now, if you take this esrog, Reb Moshe Yankel, you will get a lot of pleasure from it because it is, I assure you, a gem, one in a million."

"But is it from the island of Corfu?" my father asked, examining the esrog from every angle as one does a diamond, his hands trembling with excitement.

"What do *you* think?" the cap replied, shaking with laughter. "Nowhere else *but* from Corfu!"

My father couldn't take his eyes off the esrog, so delighted was he with it, and he summoned my mother to come and admire it, beaming as he did so as one beams at an expensive piece of jewelry or at a beloved, treasured child. My mother approached silently, slowly reaching out to touch the esrog, to hold it, but no!

"Easy with the hands! Just a sniff, if you wish."

My mother had to be content with a sniff, but I wasn't even allowed that much. I couldn't even get close enough for a look because it was considered too dangerous.

"Look who's here," said my mother. "Just give him half a chance and the next thing you know, he'll bite off the stem of the esrog and it will be spoiled for the ceremony."

"God forbid!" exclaimed my father, frightened by such awful words.

"Heaven protect us!" added the cap, its tassels bouncing.

Reb Henzel provided us with some soft flax in which to wrap the esrog, whose aroma permeated every corner of the room.

Like a diamond or a rare gemstone or a cherished heirloom which has been entrusted for safekeeping, as precious as life itself, so was the esrog treated—tenderly swaddled in flax, as one would a delicate child to protect it from becoming chilled, gently tucked into its nest of flax, and carefully placed in a fine, round wooden sugar box that had been carved and painted. The sugar had been removed with apologies to make room for the beloved guest.

"Welcome, welcome, Reb Esrog! In you go, into the sugar box." Properly blanketed with flax, covered with the lid, placed in the cupboard, the glass door shut, we bid it good night.

"I've got this terrible feeling that this mischief-maker"— meaning me—"is going to be fooling around near the cupboard, God help him, and he just might bite off the stem of the esrog!" my mother warned a second time, took me by the arm, and dragged me away from the cupboard.

Have you ever seen a cat sniffing out some cream? It springs down from the mantel, straightens out its back, paces in circles, rubs itself against the furniture, looking everyone in the eye and licking its fur. So, for a long time, Leibel hovered around the cupboard, gazing through the glass door, smiling at the box which held the esrog till his mother caught him at it and informed his father that the trouble-maker was after the esrog. So he chased Leibel off: "Back to cheder with you! Out of my sight!"

Leibel lowered his eyes and looked down at his feet and ran off to cheder.

✿   ✿   ✿

In cheder, when we studied the story of Adam and Eve, I used to wonder what would have happened had God placed them in the Garden of Eden without telling them which was the forbidden fruit. The snake would have been powerless to influence Eve to partake of the Tree of Knowledge, Eve would not have offered the apple to Adam, God would not have been angry at them, they would not have been driven from the vineyard, and we might still be strolling in the Garden of Eden to this day. The men would most likely be sitting and studying, the women would be mending socks or plucking chickens, and we boys would most likely be roaming the hills, climbing Mount Ararat, picking dates, eating pomegranates, stuffing our pockets with carob, and swimming all day in Lake Pishun.

Those suggestive words that his mother had uttered to his father, "Just give him half a chance and the next thing you know, he'll bite off the stem of the esrog," worked in Leibel like a poison, entering into his very bones.

From that moment on, the "stem of the esrog" preyed on Leibel's mind, never leaving his thoughts for a moment, coming to him in his dreams, harassing him, whispering in his ear, "Don't you recognize me, silly boy? It's me, me, the stem." Leibel would turn over on his other side and try to fall asleep again but the cajoling wouldn't stop. "Get up, silly, go open the cupboard door, take the esrog out, and bite me off. You will love my delicious taste."

In the morning, after washing up, Leibel hurried off to say his morning prayers, taking his breakfast along with him. On the way out he caught a glimpse of the box which held the esrog through the glass cupboard door and he imagined that it actually winked at him, calling out to him, enticing him, "Come here, come here, young man." Leibel ran off to cheder as fast as his legs could carry him.

One fine morning, Leibel woke up and found he was all alone in the house. His father was at the office, his mother was at the market, the girl who helped out was somewhere in the kitchen, the baby was in the cradle in a deep, smiling slumber, its little hands held alongside its head. "Angels must be playing with the baby," Leibel mused as he washed his hands, shot a quick glance at the cupboard through the glass door, and saw the box. It winked at him, called to him, tempted him. "Here! Come here, young man!" Slowly, slowly, Leibel approached the cupboard, opened the glass door, removed the box—the fine, round, wooden, carved, painted box—raised the lid, and even before he could remove the flax from the esrog, its sharp, pungent aroma assailed his nostrils, the very fragrance of the Garden of Eden. Before Leibel knew what had happened, the esrog was in his hands and the stem was staring him in the face. "Want to taste something delicious? Something out of this world? Come, bite me off! Don't be afraid, silly, no one will ever know, no one will ever tell."

Can you guess what happened? Did I bite off the stem of the esrog or did I restrain myself? I would like to know what you would have done in my place if someone had repeated ten times over that you shouldn't dare bite off the stem of the esrog. Wouldn't you be curious and want to know what the stem of an esrog tasted like?

Moshe Yankel the clerk did his work in an office and was not handy enough to build a sukkah, but his neighbor, Zalman the carpenter, was up to the job. Zalman the carpenter had plenty of lumber for the sukkah and we contributed sheets, pillowcases, and blankets with which to cover the walls. For her part, Batya Beile the clerk's wife would bake him challahs for the holidays. Zalman the carpenter was a recent widower with eight orphaned children. Batya Beile offered to help his eldest daughter, Tzivieh, make the gefillte fish, because no one in Kasrilevka could make gefillte fish like Batya Beile. And bear in mind that it was worth a good deal to have an esrog to share for the ceremony.

"You will have an equal share in the esrog with us," said Batya Beile the clerk's wife.

"Only for the blessing," Moshe Yankel the clerk hastened to correct her.

"What did you think I would do, eat it?" the carpenter retorted.

Zalman wasn't the only one who was looking forward to performing the ceremony in the sukkah. All of his children looked forward to that time as if the Messiah Himself were going to come. What a thrill it would be to hold the esrog in one hand

and the lulav in the other and to recite the blessing, *"Al nitelles lulav,"* and to shake the lulav, *Trrrrr!*

"How many days till Sukkos?" they asked one another and counted the days.

The day before Sukkos, Moshe Yankel the clerk was occupied with tying the lulav together—the palm, myrtle, and willow branches—and readying everything in the best possible way for the holiday. The decorated and bound lulav was placed by my father in a corner on top of the cupboard, leaning against the wall where it looked as if it were resting. It wasn't necessary to warn Leibel not to touch the lulav because it was too high for him to reach and even if he were to stand on a stool, nothing would come of it. The stool would likely topple over, he would come crashing down, breaking his neck, get a proper scolding, and have something to tell his grandchildren.

There was another reason why Leibel wouldn't bother the lulav. In fact, he wasn't even thinking of the lulav. All he could think of was the possibility that, God forbid, someone would find out about the stem of the esrog being bitten off. True, Leibel had immediately stuck the severed stem back on the esrog with spit, but who knew how long spit would hold? God Almighty, what would happen? What possible excuse could he give? How would he be able to look his parents in the eyes and tell an outright lie, saying that he knew nothing about it? And why did he have to do it in the first place? What good did it do him? What kind of taste does the stem of an esrog have anyway? It was—phooey!—bitter as gall, horrid, nauseating!

For nothing he had gone and ruined a holy fruit, spoiled an esrog, and such a beautiful esrog. The fruit was useless now. Of this he had been assured by his friends in cheder. Why did he have to do it? What made him do it? He was little more than a murderer, having assaulted a living thing, bitten off its head, and taken its life. Why? For what reason? What had it ever done to him? Wherever he went, he constantly saw before him the decapitated esrog, the mutilated esrog, yellow as wax, without a breath of life, a corpse, a headless corpse.

The esrog came to him in a dream, tugging at his nightshirt, wakening him, "What did you have against me? Why did you bite off my stem? Now I'm useless, useless, useless . . . !"

Leibel turned over on his other side, groaned, and fell asleep again but the voices wouldn't stop. "Murderer! What did you have against my stem? My stem . . . My stem . . ."

At last it was the first day of Sukkos. After an early morning frost, the sun rose in a clear blue sky, drenching the earth in a wonderfully joyous light that quickened one's pulse and filled one's heart with a strange feeling, that singular yearning for a summer that had fled all too quickly. The sun shone but did not warm—"like a stepmother," as they used to say in Kasrilevka. It just wasn't the same warmth as in summertime. One didn't note those special shades of green as in summertime, one didn't hear the peeping of the birds as in summertime. All, all had vanished with the first windy day of Elul, the first month of autumn. Not so quickly would the warmth of the sun return, not so quickly would that special shade of green or that peeping of the birds return. Before that time the earth would be frozen solid; before that time there would be more than enough snowstorms, cold winds, gales, and blizzards. The world would experience its annual icy upheaval before it would again awaken from its frigid slumber, cast off its frozen mantle, and clothe itself in a brand-new green garment, reviving valleys and hills, lakes and oceans, trees and flowers, wild beasts and cattle, people and fowl and all living things on earth.

On that day, Moshe Yankel the clerk arose early to look over the holiday service and to sing through the familiar holiday melodies. On that day, Batya Beile the clerk's wife arose early to prepare the holiday fish, the holiday farfel, and the holiday carrot tsimmes. On that day, Zalman the carpenter arose early to make the blessing on the esrog in the sukkah first so that he could drink his tea with milk at his leisure before dressing for the holiday.

"Reb Zalman is asking for the esrog and the lulav," my mother said to my father.

"Open the cupboard and take out the box, but be very, very careful!" my father said to her and himself placed a stool near the cupboard so that he could reach the lulav. He took the trouble to accompany the carpenter to the sukkah so that he would be present when Zalman fulfilled this important commandment.

"Here now, take it, but gently, and make the blessing on the esrog," my father told the carpenter. "In the name of God, gently."

Zalman the carpenter, God bless him, was a huge man with large hands, every finger of which was capable of knocking down three Leibels with one blow. On each giant finger was a large fingernail, always sticky with glue and stained red with shellac. When he ran his nail over a board, it left a deep furrow as if made by the sharp point of an awl. In honor of the holiday, Zalman had put on a white shirt and a new coat. He had spent hours in the bath scrubbing his hands with soap, ashes, and sand but to little avail. His hands remained sticky and his nails stained with shellac as before.

It was into these hands that the fragile, redolent esrog was entrusted. Moshe Yankel the clerk had reason to tremble with fear as Zalman the carpenter grasped the esrog, gave it a squeeze, and shook the lulav heartily.

"Easy, easy!" my father moaned worriedly. "Now, be sure to turn the esrog so the stem is on top and say the blessing, but gently, gently, for the love of God, gently."

Suddenly Moshe Yankel the clerk's body jerked back and he screamed "Oh!" in such an unnaturally loud and alarming voice that Batya Beile the clerk's wife came running into the sukkah.

"What's the matter, Moshe Yankel? May God help you!"

"You oaf! You clumsy oaf!" he screamed at the carpenter, ready to kill him on the spot. "How could you be so clumsy? What an ox! Is an esrog a hammer? A chisel? A drill? It isn't a hammer! It isn't a chisel! It isn't a drill! You've killed me as surely as if you had slit my throat! You've destroyed my esrog! Look at that poor stem—just look, you ignoramus! Clumsy ox that you are!"

We were all stunned, as if dead. Zalman the carpenter, poor man, was in a state of shock, unable to comprehend how such a calamity had occurred. How did it happen, how did the stem come off? He was almost sure that he had held the esrog ever so gently, barely touching it with his fingertips. A catastrophe! What a catastrophe! Moshe Yankel the clerk was also in a state of shock. He had not even had the chance to take the esrog to shul with him, had not even had the chance to say the first blessing over it, and already it was ruined! Why, why had he allowed such a beloved, treasured, noble fruit into such coarse, clumsy hands? Was this oaf of a carpenter too sick to go to shul and say the blessing over the community esrog?

"You clumsy oaf! You ignoramus!" Batya Beile the clerk's wife wept, wringing her hands. "Why, why did I ever believe we would have a little luck? I should have known better."

Leibel, too, was stunned, in a state of fear and remorse because of his father's woes, his mother's tears, and Zalman the carpenter's disgrace. Leibel didn't know whether to dance for joy that God had performed this miracle on his behalf, saving him from discovery and certain disaster, or whether he should cry over his father's misery, his mother's tears, and the carpenter's disgrace. Or should he throw his arms around the carpenter's neck and kiss him, kiss his calloused hands, his sticky fingers, and stained fingernails because he was his savior, his redeeming angel? Leibel glanced at his father's tragic face, at his mother's tears, at the carpenter's hands, at the esrog lying dead on the table, yellow as wax, without a stem, without a drop of life—a corpse, a headless corpse.

"A dead esrog," said my father, his voice breaking.

"A dead esrog," my mother repeated with tears in her eyes.

"A dead esrog," Zalman the carpenter echoed them, studying his hands, probably thinking, "What a pair of loathsome paws! May they wither and fall off!"

The Goldspinners

Purim is a happy holiday celebrated in the spring. The Book of Esther, which tells about the wicked Haman, is read, people exchange Purim presents of baked goods and sweets, and there are dramatized presentations of the story of Purim.

THE "Goldspinners"—who were they? Ask something easy, like how they spun gold. They were called by that name in Kasrilevka purely out of envy. They were envied, you see, because they knew how to make money. Don't get me wrong. They were poor people—may it never be your lot—just like the rest of the poor people in Kasrilevka. But when Purim came, they made money hand over fist. The Lord above had bestowed a blessing on each of them, giving to each a special talent, and the world envies people with talent. That fact is as old as the world itself. But instead of wasting any more time on these matters, we'll get right down to our story.

Naftali Long Legs was a Jew with remarkable legs which seemed to start right at his neck. Nobody could ever keep up with Naftali, not because he walked any faster but because his stride was so much longer. One moment he was right beside you and the next he was way ahead of you. Those legs were Naftali's capital, his tools of the trade, his bread and butter—in short, Naftali was a professional errand-runner.

When a wealthy landowner came to Kasrilevka once in a blue moon, Naftali would somehow get wind of it. His long legs would carry him speedily to the inn where the landowner was staying.

"My dear honorable sir, what is your wish?"

And whatever the landowner wished, Naftali would obtain it
for him in no time flat: a tailor, a shoemaker, a blacksmith, a servant, a horse, a scythe, a kettle drum, a witch, a curse on his
head—you name it! The word *no* was not in Naftali's vocabulary.
The only problem was that Naftali didn't have the field to himself. There were in Kasrilevka almost as many Jews as there were
errand-runners and more errand-runners than landowners.

Now you can understand how Naftali's legs were like money
in the bank. Nevertheless, he still would have suffered had not
God in His infinite wisdom favored His beloved people of Israel
with Purim—that joyful, lively holiday. During that joyful, lively
holiday Naftali's true talent shone forth in all its brilliance and
glory. Naftali was a born performer, and his Purim plays were
made to order for his long legs.

At first glance, you might think it ridiculous to connect Purim
plays with legs, but don't take offense if I tell you that there is
indeed a strong connection. Naftali didn't play the roles of King
Ahashuerus or Haman or Mordecai or Vashti. He played the role
of Memuchan, King Ahashuerus's chamberlain, the man who ran
the affairs of the court and palace. Whoever is acquainted with the
story of Ahashuerus knows that the role of Memuchan is a very
important one. One could even say that the whole play depends
on him. Who calls Vashti to dance before the King? Memuchan.
Who advises the King what must be done with Vashti when she
refuses to dance? Memuchan. Who arranges for Mordecai to con-
fer with Esther? Memuchan. Memuchan was here, Memuchan
was there, Memuchan was everywhere—Memuchan, Memuchan,
Memuchan! And you should have seen how our Memuchan
worked those long legs. Here's an illustration:

The door opened and in came the Purim Players with a big
"Goot yom-tov!" Naturally, all the actors had stage fright and
hung back against the wall, their arms hanging at their sides. But
our Memuchan strode out on his long legs with a sword in his
hand and a paper hat on his head. He took one long step here
and another long step there as he spouted rhymes. Let me tell
you a secret: All those rhymes spoken by Naftali which you will
hear were written by Naftali Long Legs himself:

> I, Memuchan, master of the court
> For crafty old King Ahashuerus
> (And also the master of his sport)
> Was sent to Vashti the Queen
> To command her to dance before the King
> In veils, bangles, and rings
> And other shiny, noisy things.
> > O beautiful Vashti, obey, obey,
> > The King cannot wait for you all day.

Queen Vashti (Berel Stuffnose) reluctantly tore himself from the safety of the wall and answered him, also in rhymes written by Naftali, in a whining, nasal, singsong voice, like a nervous bridegroom:

> Come hither, all ye women of Poras and Modai
> And all ye matrons of Shushan,
> Listen to my tale and sigh.
> In the Megillah I'm always put down,
> But the King is really the one to blame.
> He's a nasty drunkard without fear or shame.

Memuchan then became all fired up, pacing back and forth on his long legs, reciting rhymes of his own invention:

> What do you say to such outrageous stuff!
> Well, take it from me, I've had enough!
> If I could be sure that the King would not become upset
> I'd cut off her wicked head myself without regret.

King Ahashuerus raised his long staff, which was wrapped in gold foil:

> As far as I'm concerned, you can execute everyone
> So long as you keep the whisky handy to the throne.
> Why do all my ministers look like they've been cursed?
> Hear now! Let's all quench our thirst!
> So fill your glasses and then shout, "Hey!"
> For now we'll drink and dance and play
> Until the sunlight brings the day!

And the company joined in:

> So fill your glasses and then shout, "Hey!"
> For now we'll drink and dance and play
> Until the sunlight brings the day!

Out stepped Mordecai (Nehemiah the shoemaker), a shabby
hunchback with a beard made of flax. He knelt before the King
and then addressed Memuchan, blinking his eyes strangely
while gesticulating wildly with his hands and singing off key:

Since that day Your Majesty was left a lonely widower
Your royal word went forth alike to lord and commoner
Throughout the one hundred and twenty-seven countries of
    your kingdom
That maidens be brought before you—rich or poor,
    smart or dumb.
O my dear King! Do I have a lovely bride for you!
She's sweet as applesauce, fresh as morning dew,
Her name is Esther,
She has no brother or sister,
No father or mother,
Her nearest birthday is her twentieth,
Not counting holidays and the Sabbath . . .

Memuchan strode back and forth again with fire in his voice:

> Hurry! Hurry! Let her come before us
> To do a turn before King Ahashuerus,
> And if he takes a shine to her,
> He will place a crown on her.
> And you, Mordecai, for your matchmaking deed
> Will be given a haman-tash with poppy seed.
>   O beautiful Esther, obey, obey,
>   The King will make you his Queen today!

After the stage was set in this way, the real drama began. Naftali's
legs were stronger than iron to endure this strenuous Purim
undertaking. But out of this effort Naftali realized a nice bundle of

cash because he was, after all, the director of the troupe, its pro-
ducer, its writer, and its treasurer all rolled into one.

"He spins gold, pure gold, that man, when Purim comes!" So
said all the Kasrilevka Jews who simply envied him, not so much
for his talent as for his success in business.

If Kasrilevka consumed as much honey cake, fruit cake, and
angel cake every day of the year as it did on Purim when people
exchanged Purim gifts of baked goods, then Naftali Long Legs
wouldn't have to go through the trouble of being an errand-runner
all year and an actor on Purim. His wife, Sweet Rivella, as she
was called by everyone, would be able to support him and his
household with plenty to spare. If Naftali was famous for his
legs, then his wife, Rivella, was no less famous for her hands.

Rivella was a slightly built woman, a thin, tiny creature who,
alongside her husband, looked like a plucked chicken. To look at
her, who would believe that this little woman was capable of
supplying an entire town with sweets for Purim exchanged by
the townspeople? It's true there were other women in
Kasrilevka who were in the same business, but who possessed
such golden hands as Sweet Rivella? Her tortes and her honey
cakes, her shtrudels and angel cakes, her poppy seed cookies
and gingerbreads, her braided buns had acquired a reputation
throughout the world, even as far as Yehupotz, a neighboring
town which was in a constant rivalry with Kasrilevka. And how
did Yehupotz hear of Rivella? This is the way it happened:

There was this prankster from Kasrilevka, where there are
as many pranksters as there are stars in the sky, who decided
to play a trick by making fun of the town of Kasrilevka by, of
all things, deriding its local products. So what did this
prankster do? He mailed a package of Sweet Rivella's Purim
cakes as a Purim gift to a rich relative in Yehupotz. In the
Purim package he enclosed a letter, very nicely written, in
which he asked the rich relative to forgive him for sending
such poor stuff. The prankster added that he could find nothing worse in Kasrilevka. So imagine the prankster's surprise
when he received a thank-you note from his rich relative with
the request that he immediately buy up as much of these

baked goods as possible, pack them up properly, and send them collect to Yehupotz. (As you know, rich folks in general, and rich folks from Yehupotz in particular, love to eat and especially crave sweets.) From that time on, whole cases of Rivella's sweets were sent off each year to the rich Yehupotz relative for Purim. And that's how Rivella's fame reached even as far as Yehupotz.

But if Rivella had had to depend on the Yehupotz business alone, she would have starved. The main part of her business was in her own hometown. During the few days before Purim, Sweet Rivella was up to her ears in work. Consider: She alone had to do all the baking, all the shopping, all the wrapping, and all the negotiations with all the housewives. Just to figure up the bills for the orders required the mind of a banker! Rivella had her difficulties, especially with customers like Sarah Pearl, who was rich enough to wear pearls even on weekdays.

"You owe me, Sarah Pearl, for a half-dozen honey cakes with raisins at six groshens apiece. Six times six—how much is six times six? Isn't it thirty-three? And four almond cakes you bought at eight groshens each. It cost me seven, I swear by my health—four times eight is forty-eight. Add two large braided buns without seeds and three small braided buns with seeds and I figure these five items come to twenty-four groshens. It costs me more, may we both be well—five times twenty-four? How much is that? Let's say it was six items, then it would come to a ruble plus six groshens, but since it's five items, it must come to a ruble minus six groshens. So how much is that altogether? Let's see: Thirty-three plus forty-eight equals eight-two plus one ruble and more than half a ruble plus twenty-two minus six groshens, so how much is left? Isn't that a ruble ninety?"

"How about that! What kind of sixty-two? Where did you get sixty-two?" shouted Sarah Pearl, and both women started figuring up the amounts all over again.

"May you live and be well, Sarah Pearl, the total is exactly right: A half-dozen honey cakes with raisins at six groshens apiece is—how much is six times six? Not forty-two?"

"Congratulations! You're doing very well! Just a minute ago it was thirty-three and now it's gone up to forty-two! Not bad!"

Rivella called Naftali away from his work. He was as angry as a hornet.

"What is it with these women? They can't add two and two together. Well? Let's see your figures, but hurry, time doesn't stand still, you know!" Naftali said furiously.

Both women presented him with the figures at the same time. Naftali listened with his eyes shut, counted on his fingers and quickly became confused and angrier. He flew at his wife. "I told you a thousand times that if you don't have the brains to add two and two together, you shouldn't be selling your goods in big amounts. You should sell them one at a time! I'll show you: What do you have there? One honey cake? Give me twenty-four groshens. Another honey cake? Another twenty-four groshens. A braided bun? That's six groshens. Another bun? Another six groshens. See?"

Sarah Pearl, the rich man's wife, wasn't about to allow herself to be dealt with as if she were an ignorant pauper's wife, but she had no choice. Where else could she buy such delicious baked goods for Purim if not from Rivella? Came Purim and Rivella was the best. Everyone has his time. If you need a thief, you save him from the gallows. That's why everyone in town was so envious of her. "Golden hands . . . the gold piles up . . . both of them fill up sacks of gold when Purim comes."

Some people are blessed with beautiful singing voices, some with artistic hands, and some with dancing feet, but Noah, Naftali's eldest son, was blessed by nature with a talent for carving.

Even when Noah was a child, he was constantly being punished and nagged by his parents: "Did you ever see a boy who goes around day and night cutting and whittling and carving and carving and carving?"

In order to stop the child's nasty carving habit, they sent him to cheder and instructed the rebbi a hundred times to slap his hands if he saw him so much as holding a penknife. Better to make sure he studied the Torah. But the rebbi's efforts came to nothing. Noah left cheder with very little Torah. But he did display a rare mastery of carving. And he carved everything, whatever he laid his eyes on. There were experts in Kasrilevka who claimed that the boy possessed genius; were he to live in a big city, he would surely become . . . well, who knows *what* he might become!

Meanwhile, may his hands wither, on all the pews and all the lecterns in the synagogue, he carved figures of humans and birds and, forgive me, pigs. For carving pigs in the synagogue, Noah really caught it from his father, from his mother, from the rabbi, and from the shul elders. Whoever was offended by this deed let him have it.

"Imagine what a boy can do—in a holy place—pigs!"

But that didn't teach our carver a lesson. However, the spark glowing inside him—that heritage of his biblical ancestor, Bezalel, architect of the Great Temple—wouldn't be extinguished. His gift finally shone forth. Like all such revelations, it came about unexpectedly through a chance circumstance.

It happened a few days before Purim. He was given a wooden Purim noisemaker as a gift, the kind that children shake in their hands while the story of Purim is read in shul. Whenever the name of Haman, the villain of the Megillah, is mentioned, all the children drown out the sound of his name by making a racket with their noisemakers. Noah examined his noisemaker from every angle, quietly taking it apart and putting it together again. It occurred to him that if he only had something to do it with, he could make a noisemaker that would put all other noisemakers in the world to shame. Noah lacked only two things—material and tools, that is, wood and a knife. What to do? Well, wood was no problem. Wood could be appropriated from his mother's woodpile near the stove. But where could he get a tool, a knife? He hit on a plan. He would go to the market and sell his present noisemaker, and with the money, he would buy a knife. But a misfortune occurred. (Misfortunes always happen to innovators!) The first customer Noah approached took him by the hand and led him straight to his father. "What's going on, Reb Naftali? Your son is selling noisemakers now?"

Of course our innovator had to suffer his punishment before having a chance to explain to his father why he needed the money. Only after Noah had confessed through bitter tears what his reason was, did Naftali, after calling him a dumb ox, buy him a knife and help him select the wood. Noah sat down immediately to his work and labored so intently that in just one day, several Purim noisemakers took shape under his hands, but such extraordinary noisemakers that the whole town came to gape and to congratulate Naftali.

"It's clear, Reb Naftali, that with this son, you have nothing to worry about. He's a moneymaker already!"

From that time on, the entire town, one and all, knew that if anyone wanted the best Purim noisemaker for his money, he would have to go to Naftali's son, Noah, the carver. And no matter how much merchandise Noah prepared, it was bought up instantaneously. Every year, when Purim was over, you could hear Noah saying the same thing: "This was a great year for noisemakers!"

There was good reason for the townspeople to envy Naftali his children. "Not only does *he* earn gold and not only does *she* earn gold, pulling it in from both sides when Purim comes, but they also have to have such talented children!"

If you want to see something really nice that won't cost you much, then take a trip to our Kasrilevka at Purim time. Stop at whatever inn you like, look outside, and be prepared to see something special. From early morning on you can see boys and girls, wrapped up warmly in shawls, most of them barefoot even though it's still cold out and there are snow flurries, splashing through the mud from house to house. In their hands they are carrying large cakes or platters or bowls covered with white napkins. These are all Jewish children delivering Purim gifts which the Kasrilevka women send one another, exchanging with each other the Purim goodies prepared by Sweet Rivella.

"Itta Leah sent me two braided buns and an angel cake and two almond tortes, so I'm sending her in return one braided bun and two angel cakes and two honey cakes and one almond torte. And Yenta Mirel sent me a shtrudel and two almond breads and two poppy seed cakes and a puff cake, so I'm sending her in return two puff cakes and one almond bread and one shtrudel and two poppy seed cakes."

That's the way the Kasrilevka ladies cleverly figured and combined and balanced their exchanges so that no one would feel slighted and no one would seem too generous—in other words, an equal exchange. And since everyone in town was friendly with everyone else, there were many people exchanging Purim gifts. Even with the help of servants and one's own children, it was impossible to manage. One had to depend on others for all the exchanges. Poor boys and girls who were willing to run errands to earn Passover money were in short supply.

The luckiest were the poor people who had the most children. In Kasrilevka there were many such lucky people. But the luckiest of all were the Goldspinners, who had so many sons and daughters that it was a wonder even for Kasrilevka. I can't even tell you exactly how many they had because you're not supposed to count other people's children. May they just grow up and be healthy. What harm do they do anyone? Wintertime they huddled around the oven like little kittens, and summertime they roamed the streets playing games, raising such a cloud of dust that the street darkened and a passerby could suffocate! Fists would fly and curses were heard that would singe your ears.

But when Purim came, the children felt that they, too, were suddenly worth something—a good deal, in fact! Everyone wanted them for himself. When a Kasrilevka lady put in her baking order to Rivella, she also reserved the time of one of Rivella's children to deliver the cakes. Rivella's children were dispersed throughout the town, carrying napkin-covered trays and bowls full of baked goods. Their cheeks were flushed, their foreheads beaded with sweat, their eyes aglow with excitement. Their paths would cross in the muddy streets but they had not even a minute to stop and peek at what the other was carrying. But in passing, they would hurriedly exchange a phrase or two, so abbreviated that a stranger might not understand altogether what they were saying.

"Fatty! Where to?"

"To Big Leah's. And you, Pigeon-toes?"

"To the old lady with the long nose. Make anything?"

"Not much. And you?"

"I already have a ruble and twelve groshens. And you, how much?"

"No time to count, but more than you, I think."

"Wipe your nose!"

"Break your head!"

And they separated, each going his own way.

The Kasrilevka townspeople had been sitting at their Purim dinner tables for quite a while, singing *"Shoshanas Yaakov,"* having already heartily enjoyed Naftali Long Legs's Purim Players while Naftali's children were still running from house to house delivering Purim gifts and gathering coins from the folks, who enjoyed teasing them.

"Come here, little boy, who are you? Aren't you Naftali's boy?"

"Naftali's."

"Have you put away at least an even twenty rubles?"

"Hee-hee."

"Tell me, don't be ashamed."

"Hee-hee."

"He's giggling, hee-hee, but just look at him. You *know* he'll bring home a pocketful of gold! That's a household of goldspinners!"

All of Kasrilevka had long since gotten up from the holiday feast. Many were thinking of going to sleep, and even more were already fast asleep and snoring loudly after the brandy they had drunk in honor of the holiday which celebrated the destruction of an enemy—Haman. But one family was just sitting down to enjoy their Purim feast, slicing the large braided Purim challah and taking to the food with great good spirit. Those were the Goldspinners.

They were all hungry and tired and their legs ached but each had an interesting story to tell about his day—a raft of anecdotes! Naftali told of his Purim Players and how well they had performed that day, extraordinarily well! Only "Vashti" had stumbled over the lines.

"May he stumble from now till Passover! No matter how many times we rehearsed it so that Vashti should say, 'In the Megillah I'm always put down,' it comes out with his nasal voice, 'In the big illah I'm always but brown!' What kind of 'In the big

illah I'm always but brown'? What an idiot! May he rot! But go
talk to a stuffed-up fool . . ."

That was Naftali's story. Rivella had even funnier stories about
her customers who, it seemed, would do anything to save a little
money. One woman decided to steal a fruit cake.

"Imagine that, someone trying to steal from me!"

"'Madam, how many fruit cakes do you have there?' I asked.
She said, 'Four.' I said, 'Well, and what about the fifth?' Her face
turned red and she said to me, 'Oh, is that a fruit cake too?' So
I said, 'What did you think it was, a grandfather clock?' Said
she, 'Oh, I thought it was a honey cake!' Said I, 'So, are honey
cakes free?'"

Rivella told her stories and then Noah's turn came. His stories
had to do with noisemakers.

"This was a great year for noisemakers! Everyone wanted a
noisemaker—just noisemakers and noisemakers and noisemakers! By yesterday afternoon I was already all sold out. This one
man kept coming up to me, asking for noisemakers, so I said,
'I'm all out of noisemakers.' Said he, 'That's no excuse, you must
give me two noisemakers!' Said I, 'But where am I going to get
two noisemakers?' Said he, 'Why don't you give me your own
noisemakers?'"

"Will you ever stop with those noisemakers?!" said his father
and Noah looked down, lowered his head, and blew his nose
(under the table). That really tickled the young children. Now
it was their turn to relate adventures from their Purim gift delivering. There were so many stories to tell that it would have
taken till Passover to finish. But meanwhile, it was still Purim,
they were tired from a long day's work, and it was time to go
to bed.

The youngsters went off to their places around the stove and
soon fell into the sweet, sound sleep of happy children who have
had a full, exciting, and profitable day.

It was far into the night; Kasrilevka was long since asleep after
the great Purim feast and the Purim desserts. Only two people
in the entire town were awake and not even thinking about sleep.
They were the Goldspinners, Naftali Long Legs and Sweet

Rivella. They had quietly locked the door, drawn the curtains, and sat down with their strongbox. They wanted first to total up the coins that the little Goldspinners had brought in that lucky day, but they couldn't. They figured and figured but they could never agree; either he made a mistake or she made a mistake. Each blamed the other.

"Did you ever see such a woman who can't add two and two!" said the husband, and the wife replied, "If you're so smart, you count it, big financial expert!"

"You count it! You know better!"

"No, you count it! You know better!"

It was the time to settle the accounts and to decide what was needed for the family and what they could afford: shoes for themselves, jackets and dresses for the children—that was number one! How about matzo for Passover? How about goose fat? A crock of borscht? A sack of potatoes? It was amazing! No matter how many times they calculated, no matter how extravagant and spendthrift they wanted to be, the money was always just enough for shoes for themselves, jackets and dresses for the children, matzos for Passover, goose fat, a crock of borscht, and a sack of potatoes.

Both of their faces were flushed, their eyes glistened, their cheeks glowed, and their hearts swelled. Both of them felt that the world which God had created was, after all, not such a bad world and the people in it were, after all, not such bad people. However, it did hurt them that their own people were envious of their success. If someone else had a good day, one good day, it was so heartily resented!

"May Kasrilevka burn to the ground! A town of begrudgers!" said Naftali, and Rivella came to the defense of the town of Kasrilevka: "Poor people, for God's sake . . ."

"Poor people, she says. To her everyone is poor, heh-heh! Kasrilevka people—paupers! Beggars! Pennypinchers! Egotists!"

"Bite your tongue!" said Rivella, frightened by her husband speaking so bitterly.

From a distance they could hear the crowing of a neighbor's rooster, an old rooster with a worn-out voice. He would start enthusiastically in the upper registers but by the time he reached the low notes, his voice would give out.

"Cock-a-doodle-dooooo . . . oo . . . oo."

It almost sounded as if he were asking himself a question: "Old fool! Why are you screeching?"

The sky was beginning to turn blue. Dawn was breaking. The day was beginning.

The Passover Exiles

The weeks between Purim and Passover are spent cleaning the house from top to bottom to make sure that everything is free of any trace of chometz, *or grain and yeast products.*

"THANK God we're finished with Purim and we have just enough time to get ready for Passover."

So said my mother to herself the morning after Purim as she went poking through every corner of the parlor, turning about like a hen looking for a place to lay an egg. A few days later two wooden blocks with some hay on top suddenly appeared in a corner of the room and on the wooden blocks was a spanking-new keg of Passover borscht, covered with a thick white linen cloth. It would be left there to ferment slowly so that when Passover came, it would be ready to eat. In the meantime, it was strictly off limits.

My father and I were summoned and warned repeatedly that we shouldn't dare go near, shouldn't dare look, shouldn't dare sniff around "in that corner." Immediately thereafter, the door to the parlor was shut and both of us, my father and I, were further instructed in a firm but gentle manner to remove ourselves and whatever belonged to us from the parlor and not to return until Passover.

From that moment on, the parlor took on a most attractive character in my eyes and I was drawn to it like a magnet, longing to take a peek "into that corner," if only from afar. Standing on the other side of the door while munching on a thick slice of bread smeared with chicken fat, I peered into our sunny parlor and delighted in the tawny spruce wood sofa, shiny as a fiddle,

the three-legged semicircular table, the oval, finely beveled mirror,
and the magnificent biblical painting on the eastern wall, marking
the direction to Jerusalem, that my father himself had executed
when still a young man. My oh my! What you couldn't find in
that painting! Bears, lions, wildcats, eagles, birds, shofers, meno-
rahs, esrogs, Passover plates with Stars of David, decorative dots,
buttons, little wheels covering every inch. It was unbelievable
that a human hand could have depicted a whole world of different things, almost beyond what the eye could take in. "My father
is a genius!" I thought. "Such skill, such originality!"

"Get away from the parlor door with that bread, you rascal!
Get away immediately!"

So said my mother, grabbing my left ear with two bony fingers
as she delivered me to my father.

"Here, just look at this heir of yours. With that thick slice of
bread in his hand, he was over *there*, standing and *looking* at the
Passover borscht!"

My father put on a solemn face, shook his head, pursed his
lips, and clucked with his tongue, "Tsk-tsk-tsk! Get away from
there, you good-for-nothing!" And when my mother turned
away, a knowing smile played on my father's face, but when she
turned back, the stern look reappeared. He took me by the
hand, sat me down on a stool beside him, and told me I was not
even to look "in that corner"—it was forbidden.

"Not even from far away?"

But my father was no longer listening to me. He was already
deeply engrossed in his Bible study, chanting under his breath.
Quietly I stole off to the parlor door to peek in through a crack
at the magical room where everything was so beautiful and
clean. New pots and crockery stood on the floor, and a cleaver,
a chopping block, and two wreaths of garlic hung on the wall.

"The parlor is ready for Passover—for Passover! For
Passover!"

"Would you mind taking yourselves and your books into the
large bedroom?"

So said my mother, all dressed in white, a white kerchief on
her head, a long stick in one hand, and a new feather duster in

the other, stretching her neck and tilting her head back to inspect the ceiling.

"Sossil! Where are you hiding with that brush? Come in here, girl! Get to work!"

Sossil, the maid, her head also covered with a white cloth, made her appearance with a wet brush and a pail of whitewash. The two of them looked like ghosts in white shrouds. Sossil smeared the ceiling back and forth with wet brush: *Fliak! Fliak!* Both of them worked like angry bees.

But to stand and observe this rare comedy wasn't a pleasure long allowed me. First, I was told in no uncertain terms that a boy shouldn't be standing watching while people were whitewashing the walls for Passover. After that, the advice turned more serious.

"Look here, how's about getting back to the bedroom," my mother said, taking my arm and steering me there. But I wasn't quite ready to leave and so moved out of her reach only to bump into Sossil. Sossil immediately pushed me back to my mother:

"How come you're always underfoot?"

"Go to your father, for pity's sake!" said my mother, pushing me onto Sossil, who pushed me back to my mother, saying:

"I never saw such a pain-in-the-neck in my life!"

"Can't get rid of him!" said my mother, swatting my behind while Sossil grabbed me and daubed my face with whitewash. Dissolved in tears, I tumbled into the bedroom and into my father's arms. My father tore himself away from his studies, tried to console me as much as he could, sat me on his knee, and was soon deep in his studies again.

"I beg your pardon, sir. The madam said, would you mind moving from here into the small bedroom."

So said Sossil to my father as she came in covered with whitewash like a ghost, lugging her cleaning paraphernalia. We had to move ourselves, books and all, into the small bedroom which was no bigger than a closet. There was room enough for just one bed in which I slept with—please don't tell anybody—Sossil, the maid. Sossil was, you understand, a relative who had been with us for years and years from before the time I was born. It was in her arms I grew up, she always said. Were it not for her, she always said, I would not be alive today. Whatever ailment was going around, whatever sickness or rash, I was the first to get it, she always said, and it was she who pulled me through all those catastrophes. "Is this a way to repay me? Doesn't he deserve a spanking?" she always said.

So saying, she gave me a push or two and pulled my hair for good measure. And—would you believe it!—no one stopped her! Neither my mother nor my father took my part. Whatever Sossil wanted to do with me, she could—just as if I belonged to her and not to them.

In the small bedroom I huddled in a corner, sitting on the floor, and watched my father as he stroked his forehead, chewed on his beard, and swayed to his own drawn-out chanting of the text: "And so it is said . . ." But in came Sossil with her paraphernalia and politely told us once again to get our belongings together and move out.

"But where to?" asked my father, startled by her request.

"How do I know where?" said Sossil, standing in the middle of the room with her brush.

"Into the pantry!" said my mother and entered with her long stick now topped with the feather duster, looking like an enemy on the attack, weapon in hand.

"It's as cold as ice there now," said my father, trying to play on her sympathy.

"So freeze!" said my mother, unmoved.

"People freeze outside, not inside," added Sossil and started to splatter the dry walls with the wet brush. And we had to move ourselves from the small bedroom into the even smaller pantry where we at once began to shiver. Here it wasn't easy for my father to sit and read his books. The pantry was a tiny, crowded, dark room with barely enough space for two people. But for me it was paradise. After all, the pantry was lined with shelves—great for climbing! True, my father wouldn't let me climb on them. He said I might fall and hurt myself. But who listens? No sooner was he into his books than—aha!—I was up on the first shelf, and from the first shelf on to the second shelf, and then to the third.

"Cock-a-doodle-doo!" I crowed at the top of my lungs to show my father my great achievement. I stood up straight and cracked my head on the ceiling so hard that my teeth rattled in my head. My father was taken by surprise and cried out. Sossil, with my mother right behind her, came running and both of them gave me what for.

"How can a boy be so childish?" complained my mother.

"A boy? He's a devil, not a boy!" Sossil added, meanwhile forewarning us that we would soon be asked to move into the kitchen because the house was already more than half-ready for Passover.

There I found Moshe-Ber with the thick eyebrows sitting with my father on a bench. They were not studying now but were sharing instead their bitter experiences. My father was complaining about the Passover exile that he had been enduring for several days now.

"We're nomads, wanderers, driven from one place to the next!"

Moshe-Ber said that was nothing compared to his woes; his situation was far worse.

"My wife drove me out of the house altogether!"

I looked at Moshe-Ber with his beetle brows and could not for the life of me imagine how a man like him, so large and with such thick eyebrows, could be driven out by anyone. Little by little, the two men returned to their customary study routine and odd-sounding talk: "Rambam . . . Kuzari . . . Philosophy . . . Spinoza . . . and so forth—words that were gibberish to me.

Of far greater interest to me was the gray cat sitting on the hearth grooming herself. Sossil used to say that when a cat washed itself, it meant that we could expect a guest. Now, how does a cat know when a guest is coming? I went over and started to play with the cat. First I tried pressing down on her paw with my finger. She wasn't interested. Then I tried to teach her how to "beg" standing up on her hind legs. Still not interested.

"Sit up! Beg!" I commanded her, rapping her on the nose several times. But she only shut her eyes, turned her head aside, and stuck her little tongue out, making a peculiar face as if to say, "What does this boy want from my life? Why has he latched on to me like this?" That hurt my feelings. What a stubborn cat! I pestered her so long she scratched me with her sharp claws and I screamed out loud, "Ow-w! Ma-ama!"

My mother and Sossil came running breathlessly and they took turns scolding me, telling me I should know better than to start up with cats. To them, one measly cat is the same as "cats."

"Go wash up," my mother called out to my father, "and we'll go down to the cellar to eat supper."

Sossil grabbed a poker and started to move the pots around on the big stove without so much as a glance at me, my father, or Moshe-Ber. Soon she let Moshe-Ber know that he had no business visiting just before Passover. It seemed to make more sense, she said, for him to stay home rather than get in other people's way in their houses. Moshe-Ber took the hint and said good-bye, and we went down to the cellar for our supper.

I really couldn't see why my father was making such faces, shrugging his shoulders and muttering under his breath:

"Still wandering! Always wandering!"

What's the tragedy in eating one supper in the cellar? What's wrong with the smell of pickles, fermenting cabbage, and sour milk? What's so terrible about taking two overturned barrels, laying a noodle board across them, and using that as a table while using other barrels for chairs? Quite the opposite. To me that's a lot better and a lot more fun. That way you can roll around the cellar on the barrel. So what if you fall down? You get up and roll around again. The only problem was that Sossil had her eye on me, making sure I didn't roll myself around.

"He's thought up another trick!" she cried. "He's just dying to break an arm or a leg!"

That's ridiculous! Why would I want to break an arm or a leg? I don't know what Sossil wanted of my young life. She was constantly persecuting me, making everything seem worse than it was. If I ran, she said that I'd crack my skull. If I touched anything, she said I'd break it. If I sucked on a button, she got hysterical: "That crazy child will choke himself!" That's why I used to get even with her when I got sick. The minute I felt a little queasy, she would make a terrible fuss over me and do whatever I wanted.

"Now take the child and go upstairs. We have to clean out the last bit of bread and leaven from the cellar."

So said my mother after saying grace, and before my father could ask her where we could possibly go, she anticipated the question and said, "For a few hours up to the attic."

"Because we just washed all the floors and they are still wet," added Sossil. "Just make sure this wild one doesn't fall down the stairs and break every bone in his body."

"Bite your tongue!" my mother said sharply, and Sossil pushed me on ahead of her to get me out of the way a little faster.

"Come on, slowpoke, hurry up!"

My father walked behind me and I could hear him grumbling under his breath, "To the attic, of all places. What an exile!"

What a peculiar man my father was. He was told to go to the attic and he still wasn't happy. I don't know. If I had my way, I would like it to be Passover every week so we could climb up to the attic more often. The climb itself was a thrill. Any other day of the year, if it were my last wish on earth, they wouldn't let me make that climb. But there I was, scampering up the stairs like a demon. My father tried to catch up with me, warning, "Slow down! Be careful!"

How could I slow down? Who could even think of being careful? I felt as if I had sprouted wings like a bird and was flying. I was flying!

Do you have any idea what could be found in our attic? Treasures! Real treasures! Broken lamp globes, cracked pots, old clothes so threadbare you couldn't tell whether they were men's or women's. An old fur piece which disintegrated at the merest touch, like snow, loose pages from Hebrew texts, a burned-out samovar chimney, plumes, a rusty sieve, and an old lulav lying full length on the floor. And the beams! And the rafters! And the roof! The roof was made entirely of shingles and I could touch it with my hands. No small matter, to be able to touch a *roof* with your hands!

My father sat himself down on a plank, gathered up the loose pages of the books, and started putting them together while becoming deeply absorbed in their texts. Meanwhile, I stood next to the small attic window which overlooked the entire town of Kasrilevka, laid out below me as if on a platter—all the houses and all the roofs—black, gray, red, and green. The people down below were walking about looking like midgets and I imagined that there couldn't possibly be a better or more beautiful town than ours in the whole world. In all the courtyards I could see the townspeople washing, scrubbing, scouring, cleansing, and making things kosher. Sparing no effort, they lugged huge vats of boiling water, steam-heated irons, and hot glowing bricks from which arose a cloud of white vapor. The cloud of vapor swirled about and soon dispersed, like smoke. There was a hint of spring in the air. Little rivulets of water ran in the streets, goats bleated, and an old Jew, wearing makeshift boots held together by rope, was urging his white horse through the deep mud. That was poor Ezriel the coachman. He was whipping the horse, which could barely drag its legs through the thick mire. Ezriel was delivering a load of matzos, which reminded me that we already had our matzos a long time. They were locked away in a cupboard, covered with a white sheet. We also had a basket of eggs, a whole jar of Passover chicken fat, two wreaths of onions hanging on the wall, and many more good things for the beloved holiday. I reminded myself of the new clothes which they promised would be ready in time for Passover and my heart swelled within me.

"Sir!" a voice reached us from below. "Be so kind as to go out in the courtyard to air out the books!"

My father stood up, spitting the words out in rage. "Phoo on all this! Will this exile never end?!"

I still couldn't understand my father. Why wasn't he happy? What could be better and more exciting than to stand outside and air the books? I hurried away from the window and bolted out of the attic door and—*bumpety-bump!*—head over heels, I tumbled all the way down the stairs!

What happened next, I can't say. I only know that it took me quite some time to recover from that tumble. They say I almost didn't make it. But, as you can see, I am strong and healthy, may it never be worse. Except for a tiny scar on my face and some shortness of breath and an occasional blinking of the eyes when I speak, I'm as healthy as you.

The First Commune

L ET me tell you something: There is not a trouble in the world to which a person cannot grow accustomed. You'd think that nothing could be worse than a toothache. Nevertheless, I can cite as evidence what happened to my rebbi, Reb Monish. He used to say that were he, God forbid, to get a toothache, he would go out of his mind. And, as it is written in the Bible, thus it came to pass. The time came when a tooth of his began to ache. At first he howled unnaturally, climbed the walls, hopped about the house, and sent all the cheder children home. In the morning, when we returned to cheder, we found him moaning quietly with one cheek wrapped up and his lip swollen. On the second morning, both cheeks were wrapped up, his face glistened as if smeared with butter and he sat subdued, quiet as a mouse, not a peep out of him.

"Rebbi, what's new with your tooth?"

"*Which* tooth?" our rebbi replied with a miserable little smile. "Every one of my teeth, blessed be His name, is aching now."

I'm telling you this story so that you won't be surprised to discover that we finally became accustomed to living in Hershke Mamtzes's house, almost forgetting that we had once lived in our own house, a beautiful house with a courtyard, a garden, a sukkah, a separate pantry, and—well, you name it. True, my mother would still become tearful and let my father know that there was not so much as one inch of storage space. To this my father would respond either not at all or with a deep sigh. But if she really nagged him, showing him how in a proper household one had to have a little storage space, at least a bit of shelf for something, he would finally reply, "Don't sin. Thank God for what we have."

That was his response to everything: to the fact that three

housewives had to cook at the same stove, to the fact that all three families had to draw water from the same pump and dispose of waste in the same garbage pail, to the fact that there was only one coop for all the fowl, and to the fact that if one of the goats caused some damage, there was no way of knowing whose it was.

"I beg your pardon, Tzivieh Leah, but your goat will be the death of me. She ruined my milk bucket today," my mother complained to our landlady.

"Didn't your goat break my window pane yesterday?" retorted Tzivieh Leah, a fat woman with a deep voice.

"How do you know it was *my* goat that broke your window pane?" my mother countered.

"How do you know it was *my* goat that ruined your bucket?" replied Tzivieh Leah.

"It certainly wasn't *my* goat!" interjected the third housewife, a small woman with black eyes whose name was Perella but who was called "Sparks" because she flared up quickly and as quickly died down—exactly the opposite of her husband, whom we called "*Really* Moishe."

Those who would believe that three housewives who cook at the same stove, draw water from the same pump, and deposit refuse in one garbage can would constantly quarrel are greatly mistaken. True, it was not all love and kisses; one couldn't say that they loved one another so much that they couldn't bear to be apart. Human beings are, after all, just that—human beings. They love one another best at a distance. Those old comforting tales about how one day we will all live together as brothers, share one communal purse, beat our swords into plowshares and our weapons into pruning hooks never to wage war, never to slander or to be spiteful but to live in Utopia—that will only happen when the Messiah comes. Till that time, three housewives living together under one roof and cooking at one stove will inevitably quarrel, insult one another, and occasionally do even worse.

Of course, Tzivieh Leah, Hershke Mamtzes's wife, was a special case. She was, after all, the landlady of the house: she owned property and so expected everyone to pay her respect. You didn't dare speak to her unless you started with "I beg your pardon." She was able to have her way with my mother, who used a deferential tone with her.

"I beg your pardon, Tzivieh Leah, but the garbage pail is full to overflowing."

Or: "I beg your pardon, Tzivieh Leah, but your child has made a mess over there."

Because of my mother's tact, Tzivieh Leah thought the world of her and made sure to tell her so whenever the landlady was quarreling with Perella, the third housewife.

"Do you know, Batya, dear heart," she would say to my mother with a sweet smile, "do you know why I love you so much? Because you aren't like 'Sparks.'" Perella, getting the point, would then say to my mother, also in a voice as sweet as sugar:

"Do you know, Batya dear, why *I* love you so much? Because you don't own a shack with the paint peeling from the walls and with a leaky roof and because you don't think you are God's gift to the world."

That's how both women would complain to my mother about each other while telling her why they loved her, enumerating all of her many virtues.

My mother's greatest virtue was her genuine love of peace. She would change the subject rather than take sides.

If not for my mother, it would have been a battle royal. Even so, she was forced to witness ugly scenes, to give ear to bitter complaints, and literally to pull these two women apart when they became angry. At those times, she said, they were worse than wild beasts, ready to bite off each other's nose or scratch each other's eyes out. Only I knew how dearly it cost my mother in health. More than once I found her sitting and crying (she cried over everything), bemoaning her fate. No sooner would my father come in than she would dry her eyes as if nothing had happened.

"What's the matter?" my father would ask her anxiously.

"What do you mean, 'What's the matter'?" my mother would reply innocently.

"Why have you been crying?"

"Who, me?" My mother would try to look happy as the tears

slipped from her pretty eyes down her lovely pale cheeks. If I hadn't been embarrassed to do it in front of my father, I would have thrown my arms around her neck and kissed away every tear.

All together we were seven boys in this three-household family: Hershke Mamtzes's four sons, two red-heads and two dark-haired boys—Isaac, Itzik, Hilik, and Israelik; "*Really* Moishe"'s two boys—Yoelikel and Shoelikel; and me—Avrahamel. In addition to the seven boys there were six girls: two of Tzivieh Leah's daughters, both with blond hair—Itke and Baylke; and four of Perella's girls—Reiselleh, Foigelleh, Hannahleh, and Yentelleh.

The boys and girls fought like cats and dogs. We hated each other so much that we couldn't even stand the sight of one another. If something broke, the boys blamed the girls and the girls blamed the boys till we came to blows. The boys pulled the girls' hair and the girls screeched so loudly that Hershke Mamtzes would come running. He was an angry man who detested squabbling. With his open hand he would slap as many of us as he could reach, saying as he did so, "Pitch-potch! Down a notch!" Luckily, "*Really* Moishe" would intercede and yank the boys out of Hershke Mamtzes's reach.

"Let's *really* put an end to this now!"

He was a curious fellow, this "*Really* Moishe"—a man with a childlike soul. He could spend entire days and nights with us children, helping us to make, build, put together, or take apart things. It goes without saying that when it came to puttering, "*Really* Moishe" was something of a master craftsman. How could he stand by and simply watch while someone else was whittling, sawing, or making something?

"Here, give it to me, you good-for-nothing, and I'll show you how you *really* use a whittling knife!"

But that was nothing. Just between us, "*Really* Moishe" never thought it beneath him to tuck the hem of his long coat into his belt and join us kids in a game of hide-and-go-seek, Johnny-jump-up, or hopscotch. And playing with him was, I tell you, a treat. So what did God do? He gave him a wife, Perella, who didn't let him play with us. What a tragedy!

✿   ✿   ✿

It has long been known that all great ideas come about unexpectedly, as if by chance. And so it was with the idea for the commune, which was born unexpectedly, quite by chance. This is how it happened. Soon after Purim, the grownups were figuring out how much flour each family would need for Passover matzos, and an extraordinary coincidence came to light. It soon became plain that we all needed the same amount, no more nor less. Here's how it added up: My mother, my father, and I were three. We were expecting guests—my older sister, Asna; her husband, Daniel; and their three children—from a small town in Bessarabia, so you have a total of no less than eight people. Figure Hershke Mamtzes and his wife and their four sons and two daughters—there again you have exactly eight. Now take "*Really* Moishe" with his wife, two boys, and four girls—again eight.

"Wonder of wonders! A miracle from heaven!" the men exclaimed jokingly.

"It's got to be Fate!" the women added, more seriously.

"Listen to this, my friends, I have an idea. Wouldn't it make sense if for these eight days of Passover we would all join forces and celebrate together?" I think it was "*Really* Moishe" who said that, and Hershke Mamtzes added immediately:

"Yes, kind of a partnership, it's known as a cooperative, but whatever you call it, let's do it together."

"Some people call it a commune," my father contributed, and "*Really* Moishe" presented us with an explanation illustrated by gestures:

"Commune means: What's mine is yours, what's yours is mine—one pot, one purse, one voice."

"And especially on Passover," all the men said at once, "when all Jews eat one bread—the simple matzo—when all of us drink the same raisin wine—four glasses full—when we all eat the same green vegetables and horseradish, and when all of us recite from the same Haggadah. Passover is really the best holiday. On Passover, all Jews would do well to have a commune."

The men glanced furtively at their wives—what would they say to this plan? But the wives wisely kept their silence. They were probably thinking, "Why should we stick our necks out? You men want a commune, so have a commune. If it doesn't work out, you can't blame us." In short, the women worked it out rather diplomatically, as women generally do, and the plan for the commune was adopted—not all at once, but gradually.

First of all the three women together bought a sack of flour and baked their matzos at one time at the bakers. This year the matzos turned out better than ever. They brought the matzos home and wished one another well, hoping that they and their husbands and children would all live and be well till the next year when they would bake matzos together again. It was so heartwarming to observe the camaraderie and affection among the wives, as if they had never bickered, never gossiped or even so much as exchanged an angry word. Not just the women, but the men and we youngsters that day felt happier than we had since we started living together under one roof. It was a miracle. Even Hershke Mamtzes, who was always in a bad mood and grumbling at the world (because at one time his in-laws had tried to take his house away from him), this day was unusually genial; he didn't smack us, saying, as was his habit, "Pitch-potch! Down a notch!" and was even humming to himself. Even Tzivieh Leah's voice was that day somehow lighter and softer. In a word, a good angel had alighted on Hershke Mamtzes's house. Its spirit descended on the household.

Having finished with the matzos, the women together put up a crock of Passover borscht, the crock provided, naturally, by "*Really* Moishe," and again they wished one another well, hoping that they and their husbands and children would all live and be well till the next year when they would put up a Passover borscht together again. The house was filled with a happy holiday spirit. After that they all bought a number of chickens and two turkeys. God had provided a real bargain. A crazy peasant was asking only ten gulden for the two turkeys, which were as big as calves. They tossed all the chickens into one coop (repaired, naturally, by "*Really* Moishe"). The turkeys were allowed to roam free about the house, and for us children it became a great game. We chased the turkeys, teased them, and whistled at them as they squawked, "Gobble-gobble!"—and no one stopped us. The wives again wished one another well, hoping that they and their husbands would all live and be well till the next year when they would buy such excellent chickens and turkeys for Passover together again.

They then bought three sacks of potatoes for cash and dozens
of eggs at a low price—three gulden a dozen. God had sent
them a peasant woman with eggs—God bless her—and the
wives laughed at the silly woman as again they wished one
another well, hoping that they and their husbands and children
would all live and be well till the next year when they would buy
such fresh eggs together again.

Need I go on? A sack of Passover coals for the samovar was
purchased for a song, it's a shame to say for how little; horseradish and parsnips—all at half-price. "A Passover of real bar-
gains!" the women declared as they laughed, and we young folk
whistled at the turkeys and the turkeys answered, "Gobble-
gobble!" It was obviously the greatest idea in the world to be
working together as one.

"Commune? You ladies have been playing at commune?" the
men teased.

But the women said straight out that they wouldn't mind having
"commune" all year round. They were in favor of the idea, the
men certainly were, and we children—well, what do *you* think!

Only the fish, the meat, and the wine remained to be bought
on the last day. Who else but "*Really* Moishe" took it upon
himself to buy the fish because where in the world could you
find such an expert when it came to buying fish? He would
bring home fish that were *really* fish! The wine, chopped
apples, and nuts were left entirely to my father as he was the
wine specialist. The koshering of the dishes and silverware
were assigned to the boys; the girls were given other chores:
helping their mothers to scrub, scour, and polish. We boys
rolled up our trousers and went off to the pond with the
dishes, happy and excited. In short, it was a merry time, all of
us busy, all hands occupied, no one with a moment to spare as
we disposed of the last of the ordinary bread, went to the bathhouse, came home, dressed in our holiday clothes, and began
the preparations for the seder.

As you would expect, "*Really* Moishe" set up the tables
and chairs, laid out the wineglasses and silverware, and arranged
pillows in heaps on the men's chairs. These were the hesev-beds,

which, according to Passover tradition, would permit them to recline on their elbows like kings of old. Anyone who missed "*Really* Moishe"'s bustling around that evening, missed something *really* special. His cheeks were flushed, his hat had slipped down over his ear, and one half of his moustache, the long side, seemed to hang down farther. He looked like the captain of a ship, the general of an army. He wouldn't allow anyone else to touch a thing. By himself he carried in the chairs, by himself he set out the wineglasses, the salt water, the chopped apples and bitter greens. By himself he prepared the four chairs for the men to recline on (my brother-in-law, Daniel, was also counted among the men). When it came to the heaps of pillows, he ordered us to bring in more and more pillows.

"More pillows!"

"Here's another one!"

"More pillows!"

"Here's another one!"

"More pillows!"

"Why do you need so many pillows?"

"More!"

Four tall mounds of pillows grew before our eyes. Did I say mounds? Four tall *towers,* so tall that when the four men returned from shul, they literally had to scramble up to the top, and when they reached the top and were seated, they were afraid they might fall off.

The first to climb up was our landlord, Hershke Mamtzes. He didn't complain at all about the height of the pillows; he just shrugged and muttered angrily, "Wh-what a hesev-bed!"

"Ha! That's *really* a hesev-bed!" Moishe cried out to him with the satisfied smile of a great artist who is proud of his work.

"Let's just hope it doesn't wind up like your sukkah," retorted the landlord sarcastically.

"I was thinking the same thing," said my father, clambering onto the cushions, holding on to his belt with both hands and stamping down the cushions as one does hay on a wagon.

"If you want something done, do it yourself," interjected the landlady spitefully, and "Sparks," defending her husband, said to Moishe angrily:

"You always have to show off, don't you? I wouldn't lift a finger to fix up their pillows. Let them do it themselves!"

Understandably, Tzivieh Leah wasn't going to let this go unanswered and so she said to my mother in an artificial tone:

"Do you see, Batya, dear heart, 'Sparks' are flying already."

And "Sparks" leaned over to my mother and whispered in her ear for all to hear, "Do you hear, Batya, my love, the tea kettle, praised be God, is boiling already."

All of us could sense that a cloud was slowly descending on Hershke Mamtzes's house. The happiness and the liveliness that had prevailed before Passover was disappearing—vanishing, vanishing with the wind and the smoke.

"May you both be strong and healthy, Tzivieh Leah, I beg your pardon, and Perella, honey. Don't forget that it's yom-tov, a holiday, and we are sitting together at one table," my mother said softly, and her face was so full of sorrow and anguish that my heart almost broke.

I had noticed during the candle blessing that she was crying—crying for her own house, the one we had lost, crying because we had to share the holidays with such crude people and had to sit with them at one table, at one seder. Just a year ago we had a little nicer table, a little richer seder. A year ago my father was the only king and my mother was the only queen and I was the only prince. Today, all crowded together were several kings, several queens, and many, many princes, and all the princes were dressed up in holiday clothes as fine as mine and perhaps a little finer. No, say what you will, it wasn't the same as last year's Passover. It wasn't last year's seder.

Even though there were many princes sitting at the table and all were dressed up for the holidays as nicely as I was and perhaps a little nicer, nevertheless I felt that I was set apart from the others. Even though there were several kings and several queens, nevertheless I felt that my father and my mother were not like the other mothers and fathers. If the others were kings, then he was a king above the other kings because he was the handsomest and the most refined of them all. My father recited from the Siddur, conducting the ceremony like an elder, like a general, and everyone looked to him to know what to do next. Even my mother set an example for the women as she read her own fat prayer book and turned the pages with her slender fingers as her pale face glowed like the sun. Picture it: Even my sister, Asna, not a bad-looking woman, couldn't hold a candle to my mother. What a pity that from all her crying, she had developed dark circles under her eyes. What a pity that from all the cooking and scrubbing, her pretty hands had become calloused. What a pity that because of my sister Asna's wedding, she'd had to sell her rings, pearls, and earrings and couldn't show off her true beauty. We praise the beauty of Rachel, Queen Esther, Shulamit from the "Song of Songs," the Queen of Sheba—but they are just fantasies. Give my mother back her rings, her pearls, and her earrings and then you will see true beauty! But it's no use. The rings are gone! The pearls are gone! The earrings are gone! Gone! Sold!

"Kid-duu-shh!" chanted the king of kings—my father, that is—as he sat up with difficulty from his pile of pillows and held his wineglass in one hand while supporting himself on the table with the other. He tilted his head back, shut his eyes, and began the beautiful Passover benediction over the wine with its moving Passover variation—but with a certain sorrowful intonation. No, it was not the same melody he sang a year ago at Passover. I imagined that in my father's kiddush I could hear a plea to the Heavenly Court of Judgment, a plea for our old house, for my mother's rings and her pearls and her earrings, and for all the other troubles, griefs, and heartaches that God had dealt us this year with His broad hand.

Like all great ideas, so too the greatest misfortunes that occur in the world often start with a trifle, a foolish incident. So it was that the commune I'm telling you about had its sudden downfall at its very birth over nothing, over a foolish incident. This is how it happened.

As soon as my father finished saying the kiddush and sank back onto his heap of pillows, both my brother-in-law, Daniel, and our landlord, Hershke Mamtzes, each thinking it was his turn to say the kiddush next, stood up at the same time, then hastily sat down again, their faces reddening with embarrassment.

My father indicated to Hershke Mamtzes by sign language and sounds (because during the kiddush you aren't supposed to speak), "Nu-oh!" That meant he would be honored if he would make the kiddush next. Hershke Mamtzes replied, motioning with his hand to my brother-in-law, Daniel, "Ee-oh!" That meant, "Look at that young upstart, thinking he's old enough to say the kiddush." My brother-in-law responded with a shake of the head, "Ee-ee!" That meant, "Let someone else make the kiddush next." "*Really* Moishe" put in his two cents' worth (he always loved to get into the act) and gestured with his hand, "Me-oh-nu!" Translated, that meant, "Make up your minds, one or the other." My father replied with a wink of the eye and a "Ma-oh-ee!" meaning, "If not this one or that one, then *you* make the kiddush first."

I don't know what was so funny about all this, but we children suddenly found that we couldn't keep from laughing—and what laughter it was! We suppressed it behind our hands, afraid to look at one another lest we burst out laughing. But how long can a human being control himself? A human being is not made of iron, particularly when he is surrounded at the table by so many silly, noisy, mischievous no-goods who know what it means to laugh. It didn't take much more than a hiccup or a cough to make any one of us lose control. At such moments, I tell you, it was awful; we were playing with fire, because the more we held it in, the more likely we were to explode. You can prove it with your own friends. Just make one rule—no laughing at the table—and you'll see what will happen. At first they'll try to hold it in as long as possible and then there will be such an outburst of laughter that you'll finally burst out laughing yourself. I don't have an explanation for this; I'll leave it to the experts to explain this phenomenon, while we return to our kiddush.

With God's help, the kings completed the kiddush and it was now the children's turn. Hershke Mamtzes's eldest son, Isaac, stood up and started to chant in a choked voice as if someone were strangling him. So his younger brother, Itzik, let out a little high-pitched "*Kchi!*" This made the third brother, Hilik, laugh

out loud, and he was followed by the little one, Israelik, and after
them by the rest of us. Isaac was caught right in the middle.
There was no going back or forward. It was painful to look at his
flushed, anguished face. Hershke Mamtzes sprang to his feet
and slapped him on top of his head and sent him away from the
table, saying, as was his custom, "Pitch-potch! Down a notch!"
and motioned to Itzik to stand up and make the prayer.

Itzik jumped up like a demon and started to recite the same
prayer, but so loudly and so eagerly that he was startled by his
own voice and tried to lower it by a tone. One of the bunch went
"Hic!" which made Itzik unable to speak at all because he
started to choke. So the poor boy got slapped on the head by his
father, Hershke Mamtzes, the same punishment as for Isaac,
along with the "Pitch-potch! Down a notch!" and before we
knew it, the third son, Hilik, was standing in his place.

Now this Hilik got halfway through the prayer and couldn't go
on. Somehow his eye was caught by my brother-in-law's three
children and when he saw the three of them holding their noses,
blowing up their cheeks like chipmunks, he was at the point of
exploding. And in this way, one after another, each child
received his punishment from Hershke Mamtzes—"Pitch-
potch! Down a notch!" and had to surrender his place to the
next one. Finally it came to "Really Moishe"'s children, to
Yoelikel and Shoelikel. When Yoelikel got up to recite the
prayer, he couldn't even get out the very first word, and dissolved in laughter right on the spot. Everyone started to giggle.
Big and small were laughing: my mother and my father and
"Really Moishe" and all the women. I imagined that even the
wineglasses, the dishes, the spoons, the lamp, and the walls—
everyone and everything—were gripped by laughter.

Only Hershke Mamtzes with the angry eyes was not laughing.
He allowed Yoelikel to laugh a little longer, then stood up
angrily and—apparently forgetting that Yoelikel had a father of
his own, may he live to be one hundred and twenty years, a
father who also had hands and could deal with his son as he saw
fit—slapped Yoelikel on top of the head, along with the same
"Pitch-potch! Down a notch!" as with his own sons. The whole
gathering sat stunned. Naturally, this incident mostly inflamed

Yoelikel's mother, "Sparks," whose eyes flashed as she said to Tzivieh Leah:

"Could you please inform your husband that his hands should only wither?"

It didn't take Tzivieh Leah long to think of an answer. She said to "*Really* Moishe" in her deep voice:

"Could you please inform your wife that her nasty mouth should only shrivel?"

I can't describe what then took place. I mean, I can, but I don't want to. It's not fitting . . . better to be silent.

The following day, at the second seder, each family sat separately at its own table and celebrated the seder as God commanded. Although still having to sit together in one room, in Hershke Mamtzes's living room, they made sure to turn their backs to one another, in a huff. They could hardly wait till the last day of Passover in order to divide up the remaining matzos, the chicken fat, the eggs, the potatoes, and the green vegetables. Even the crock of borscht had to be poured into separate pots. The women lost no opportunity to blame one another or to insult the men.

"Communes they wanted! Madmen invented them and idiots follow blindly! Communes! May all our enemies live in communes!"

After Passover, my father explored the entire city, looking for another house to rent, and "*Really* Moishe" soon followed suit. Tzivieh Leah suddenly softened her manner and Hershke Mamtzes said casually that immediately after Shevuos, we should all live and be well, he would start repairing the leaky roof. But it didn't help one bit. My mother told my father that under no circumstances would she remain in this house, even for free. She would rather, God forbid, live in the street than in Hershke Mamtzes's house.

And that's what became of the first commune in Kasrilevka.

Glossary

Borscht: A soup made of cabbage and beets at Passover, usually allowed to ferment for several days in a crock or keg.

Carob: A sweet wild pod, also known as St. John's bread.

Challah: The braided Sabbath or holiday egg bread.

Chanukah: The Festival of Lights celebrated for eight days in December. Commemorates the successful revolt of the Maccabees against the Syrians in 165 B.C.E.

Cheder: Room in the rebbi's house where children were taught Hebrew, prayers, and the Bible.

Chometz: Any foodstuff made from grain or yeast products. Before the start of Passover, every remnant of this must be removed from the house.

Dreydl: A four-sided spinning top, played with by children during Chanukah.

Esrog: A large, lemonlike aromatic citrus fruit, used together with the lulav (see below) in the synagogue procession during Sukkos, at which time it is blessed. The stem or apex is the most important part of the fruit, for if it breaks off the esrog is no longer considered to be valid for the religious purpose.

Farfel: Noodle dough, in pellets.

Gefillte fish: Holiday fish croquettes made of spiced ground fish.

Haggadah: Book of the Passover home service read during the two consecutive seders on the first two nights of Passover. It starts with the youngest child asking the head of the family the Four Questions. The answers relate the story of the exodus of the persecuted Jews from Egypt and their subsequent liberation.

Haman-tash: Three-cornered, filled cake eaten at Purim.

Hesev bed: The heap of soft pillows that men lean on during the seder at Passover.

Kaddish: Prayer recited by mourners after the death of a close relative.

Kiddush: Blessing recited over the wine at the beginning of the Sabbath or holiday evening meal.

Kosher: Food or drink that Jews are permitted to eat when proper special regulations have been followed in its preparation.

Latkes: Potato pancakes, traditionally eaten during Chanukah.

Lulav: Palm branch, tied together with sprigs of myrtle and willow, used together with the esrog during Sukkos to symbolize the harvest.

Matzo: Traditional unleavened flatbread eaten during Passover to commemorate the years the Jews spent wandering through the desert.

Mezuzah: Rolled-up piece of parchment inscribed with passages from Deuteronomy, placed in a container and nailed in a slanting position to the right-hand doorpost of Jewish homes and synagogues. A devout Jew will kiss his fingers and touch the mezuzah upon entering a building.

Megillah: The Book of Esther, the story of Purim, written on a scroll and read aloud in synagogue. Whenever the name of Haman, the villain of the story, is read, the children drown out the sound of it with noisemakers.

Menorah: Candelabrum holding candles for Chanukah.

Passover: Festival celebrated for eight days, commemorating the Jews' exodus from Egypt where they were slaves. Generally takes place in April.

Purim: A March festival, celebrating the downfall of Haman, the villain who tried to destroy the Jews, as told in the Book of Esther. A joyous holiday, marked by parades and costume parties, gift exchanges and dramatic renditions of the Purim story.

Reb: Mister, a respectful term for a man.

Rebbi: A teacher, generally of the children in the cheder.

Rebbitzin: The rabbi's wife.

Rosh Hashanah: Jewish New Year.

Seder: Passover celebration of the first and second evenings at which the Haggadah is read around the family supper table. The Four Questions are asked and answered; the Passover story is told; four glasses of wine are drunk; matzos, chopped apples, and bitter greens are eaten to symbolize various aspects of the history of the Jews fleeing Egypt.

Shabbos: Sabbath, starting at sundown Friday night and ending at sundown Saturday night. The day of rest and worship for Jews.

Shamesh: Candle used to light the other candles of the menorah during Chanukah.

Shevuos: The Feast of Weeks, a religious harvest holiday.

Shochet: Ritual slaughterer.

Shul: Synagogue, prayer room.

Siddur: Prayer book.

Sukkah: Home-made shed or lean-to behind the house, made of crude lumber and topped with green branches in which the family eats its meals during Sukkos. It symbolizes the dwellings used by the Jews during their wanderings in the desert.

Sukkos: The fall harvest festival, commemorating the Jews' living in crude shelters (see above) during their wanderings.

Tsimmes: Vegetables simmered with honey or sugar.

Yarmulke: Prayer cap worn by Jewish males.

Yahrtzeit: Anniversary of a person's death.

A CATALOG OF SELECTED
DOVER BOOKS
IN ALL FIELDS OF INTEREST

A CATALOG OF SELECTED DOVER
BOOKS IN ALL FIELDS OF INTEREST

CONCERNING THE SPIRITUAL IN ART, Wassily Kandinsky. Pioneering work by father of abstract art. Thoughts on color theory, nature of art. Analysis of earlier masters. 12 illustrations. 80pp. of text. 5⅜ x 8½. 23411-8

ANIMALS: 1,419 Copyright-Free Illustrations of Mammals, Birds, Fish, Insects, etc., Jim Harter (ed.). Clear wood engravings present, in extremely lifelike poses, over 1,000 species of animals. One of the most extensive pictorial sourcebooks of its kind. Captions. Index. 284pp. 9 x 12. 23766-4

CELTIC ART: The Methods of Construction, George Bain. Simple geometric techniques for making Celtic interlacements, spirals, Kells-type initials, animals, humans, etc. Over 500 illustrations. 160pp. 9 x 12. (Available in U.S. only.) 22923-8

AN ATLAS OF ANATOMY FOR ARTISTS, Fritz Schider. Most thorough reference work on art anatomy in the world. Hundreds of illustrations, including selections from works by Vesalius, Leonardo, Goya, Ingres, Michelangelo, others. 593 illustrations. 192pp. 7⅛ x 10¼. 20241-0

CELTIC HAND STROKE-BY-STROKE (Irish Half-Uncial from "The Book of Kells"): An Arthur Baker Calligraphy Manual, Arthur Baker. Complete guide to creating each letter of the alphabet in distinctive Celtic manner. Covers hand position, strokes, pens, inks, paper, more. Illustrated. 48pp. 8¼ x 11. 24336-2

EASY ORIGAMI, John Montroll. Charming collection of 32 projects (hat, cup, pelican, piano, swan, many more) specially designed for the novice origami hobbyist. Clearly illustrated easy-to-follow instructions insure that even beginning papercrafters will achieve successful results. 48pp. 8¼ x 11. 27298-2

THE COMPLETE BOOK OF BIRDHOUSE CONSTRUCTION FOR WOODWORKERS, Scott D. Campbell. Detailed instructions, illustrations, tables. Also data on bird habitat and instinct patterns. Bibliography. 3 tables. 63 illustrations in 15 figures. 48pp. 5¼ x 8½. 24407-5

BLOOMINGDALE'S ILLUSTRATED 1886 CATALOG: Fashions, Dry Goods and Housewares, Bloomingdale Brothers. Famed merchants' extremely rare catalog depicting about 1,700 products: clothing, housewares, firearms, dry goods, jewelry, more. Invaluable for dating, identifying vintage items. Also, copyright-free graphics for artists, designers. Co-published with Henry Ford Museum & Greenfield Village. 160pp. 8¼ x 11. 25780-0

HISTORIC COSTUME IN PICTURES, Braun & Schneider. Over 1,450 costumed figures in clearly detailed engravings–from dawn of civilization to end of 19th century. Captions. Many folk costumes. 256pp. 8⅜ x 11¾. 23150-X

CATALOG OF DOVER BOOKS

THE STORY OF THE TITANIC AS TOLD BY ITS SURVIVORS, Jack Winocour (ed.). What it was really like. Panic, despair, shocking inefficiency, and a little heroism. More thrilling than any fictional account. 26 illustrations. 320pp. 5⅜ x 8½.
20610-6

FAIRY AND FOLK TALES OF THE IRISH PEASANTRY, William Butler Yeats (ed.). Treasury of 64 tales from the twilight world of Celtic myth and legend: "The Soul Cages," "The Kildare Pooka," "King O'Toole and his Goose," many more. Introduction and Notes by W. B. Yeats. 352pp. 5⅜ x 8½.
26941-8

BUDDHIST MAHAYANA TEXTS, E. B. Cowell and others (eds.). Superb, accurate translations of basic documents in Mahayana Buddhism, highly important in history of religions. The Buddha-karita of Asvaghosha, Larger Sukhavativyuha, more. 448pp. 5⅜ x 8½.
25552-2

ONE TWO THREE . . . INFINITY: Facts and Speculations of Science, George Gamow. Great physicist's fascinating, readable overview of contemporary science: number theory, relativity, fourth dimension, entropy, genes, atomic structure, much more. 128 illustrations. Index. 352pp. 5⅜ x 8½.
25664-2

EXPERIMENTATION AND MEASUREMENT, W. J. Youden. Introductory manual explains laws of measurement in simple terms and offers tips for achieving accuracy and minimizing errors. Mathematics of measurement, use of instruments, experimenting with machines. 1994 edition. Foreword. Preface. Introduction. Epilogue. Selected Readings. Glossary. Index. Tables and figures. 128pp. 5⅜ x 8½.
40451-X

DALÍ ON MODERN ART: The Cuckolds of Antiquated Modern Art, Salvador Dalí. Influential painter skewers modern art and its practitioners. Outrageous evaluations of Picasso, Cézanne, Turner, more. 15 renderings of paintings discussed. 44 calligraphic decorations by Dalí. 96pp. 5⅜ x 8½. (Available in U.S. only.)
29220-7

ANTIQUE PLAYING CARDS: A Pictorial History, Henry René D'Allemagne. Over 900 elaborate, decorative images from rare playing cards (14th–20th centuries): Bacchus, death, dancing dogs, hunting scenes, royal coats of arms, players cheating, much more. 96pp. 9¼ x 12¼.
29265-7

MAKING FURNITURE MASTERPIECES: 30 Projects with Measured Drawings, Franklin H. Gottshall. Step-by-step instructions, illustrations for constructing handsome, useful pieces, among them a Sheraton desk, Chippendale chair, Spanish desk, Queen Anne table and a William and Mary dressing mirror. 224pp. 8⅛ x 11¼.
29338-6

THE FOSSIL BOOK: A Record of Prehistoric Life, Patricia V. Rich et al. Profusely illustrated definitive guide covers everything from single-celled organisms and dinosaurs to birds and mammals and the interplay between climate and man. Over 1,500 illustrations. 760pp. 7½ x 10⅛.
29371-8